COLLECTION MANAGEMENT

POLITICAL PROFILES

ARNOLD SCHWARZENEGGER

Political Profiles
Arnold Schwarzenegger

Jeff C. Young

MORGAN REYNOLDS
PUBLISHING
Greensboro, North Carolina

POLITICAL PROFILES

Barack Obama
Hillary Clinton
John McCain
Nancy Pelosi
Al Gore
Rudy Giuliani
Arnold Schwarzenegger

POLITICAL PROFILES: ARNOLD SCHWARZENEGGER
Copyright © 2008 by Jeff C. Young

Library of Congress Cataloging-in-Publication Data

Young, Jeff C., 1948-
    Political profiles : Arnold Schwarzenegger / by Jeff C. Young. -- 1st ed.
    p. cm.
    Includes bibliographical references and index.
    ISBN-13: 978-1-59935-050-9
    ISBN-10: 1-59935-050-5
    1. Schwarzenegger, Arnold--Juvenile literature. 2. Governors--California-
-Biography--Juvenile literature. 3. California--Politics and government--1951-
--Juvenile literature. 4. Bodybuilders--United States--Biography--Juvenile lit-
erature. 5. Actors--United States--Biography--Juvenile literature. I. Title. II.
Title: Arnold Schwarzenneger.
    F866.4.S38Y685 2007
    979.4'054092--dc22
    [B]
                                            2007020841

Printed in the United States of America
First Edition

*To my longtime friend, Richard H. Ernstes, whose
monogram appears on every baseball scoreboard*

Contents

Arnold Schwarzenegger
(Courtesy of AP Images)

one
My Fellow Americans

A rnold Schwarzenegger had faced many obstacles in his life, but the challenge facing him in August of 2004 was one of the biggest. He knew many of the journalists and other observers waiting for him to appear were asking one question: Could a novice politician who spoke heavily accented English deliver a stirring speech at the 2004 Republican National Convention?

The famed bodybuilder, turned actor, turned politician, had been governor of California for less than a year. The hall would be filled with a friendly crowd of the party faithful, but an additional 30 million television viewers would closely scrutinize his words, gestures, and delivery.

Schwarzenegger prepared for the speech with the same zeal and dedication that had characterized his life. For several weeks he had met with his speechwriters and other staffers to put his ideas and concepts into the right words. When his moment arrived, Schwarzenegger was prepared.

The first three sentences of the address succinctly summed up his life and the foundation of his political beliefs:

> My fellow Americans, this is an amazing moment for me. To think that a once scrawny boy from Austria could grow up to become governor of California and stand in Madison Square Garden and speak on behalf of the President of the United States—that is an immigrant's dream. That is the American dream.

Then Schwarzenegger reminded the audience of how well his adopted country had treated him. To a cynical viewer, it might have seemed that he was pandering to a partisan audience. But to anyone aware of Schwarzenegger's humble origins, the words had a ring of absolute sincerity and authenticity. "I was born in Europe and I've traveled all over the world," Schwarzenegger said. "I can tell you that there is no place, no country, more compassionate, more generous, more accepting and more welcoming than the United States of America."

As an actor and performer, Schwarzenegger instinctively knew when he had the audience's complete attention. He kept it throughout his twenty-three minute speech.

There were some exaggerations in the speech. Schwarzenegger claimed that as a child in Austria he saw Soviet tanks in the streets. But when Schwarzenegger was born, there was no Soviet occupation of the province he lived in. It was controlled by the British. He further claimed that Austria had a Socialist government after the Soviet occupation ended. In fact, the country was ruled by a coalition government.

But those misrepresentations didn't detract from his overall themes—his love for his adopted country and his stalwart support of President George W. Bush.

Schwarzenegger delivers a speech at the 2004 Republican National Convention. *(Courtesy of AP Images/Paul Sancya)*

An unspoken idea was that perhaps someday, Arnold Schwarzenegger could be speaking as the president, instead of for the president—but this could only happen if his fellow Americans decided to change the U.S. Constitution.

Schwarzenegger concluded his speech by once again addressing his audience as "my fellow Americans," and he reminded them, "I want you to know that I believe with all my heart that America remains 'the great idea' that inspires the world. It is a privilege to be born here. It's an honor to become a citizen here. It is a gift to raise your family here, to vote here and to live here."

As Schwarzenegger walked away from the podium, the thunderous applause told him that he had successfully met another challenge.

two
Second Son

When Arnold Schwarzenegger was born, his Austrian homeland had been conquered twice in seven years. In 1938, German troops seized the country and made it part of Adolf Hitler's Nazi empire. Then in 1945, the Allied powers drove out the Nazis and divided the country into four zones controlled by American, French, Soviet, and British soldiers.

Arnold, the second son and last child of Gustav, a village police chief, and Aurelia, a housewife, was born in Thal, a small village near Graz, Austria on July 30, 1947. When he was born the years of war and foreign occupation had taken a heavy toll on the country. Although Gustav had a steady job and free housing, the Schwarzeneggers didn't have indoor plumbing, a telephone, or a refrigerator in their humble home until Arnold was fourteen.

Growing up in such austere surroundings made Arnold yearn for a better life and gave him a fierce determination

Map of Austria

to excel and to become a leader. "Ever since I was a child, I would say to myself, 'There must be more to life than this," he told an interviewer. "I wanted to be different. I wanted to be part of the small percentage of people who were leaders, not the large mass of followers."

Gustav was a stern and domineering father, often cold and unaffectionate. He enjoyed pitting Arnold against his older brother Meinhard in athletic competitions. The winner received their father's temporary favor. Gustav would coldly face the loser and ask: "Tell me, which one of you is the best?"

Gustav also pushed his sons to cultivate an interest in the arts and music. On Sundays there were mandatory family trips to museums. Arnold would have preferred going to a movie. After their visit, Gustav would order his sons to write a ten-page report on what they saw. "He would correct it all over the place," Arnold recalled. "'This sentence makes no sense. Write this word fifty times. You made a mistake.'"

While Gustav was stingy with his praise, he was generous with his rules and punishments. He was physically abusive, but

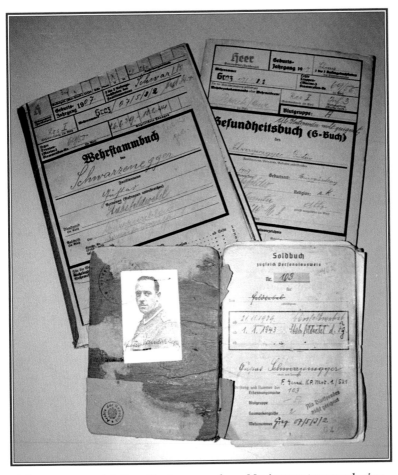

Schwarzenegger's father, Gustav, served as a Nazi storm trooper during WWII. This photo of Gustav was found among his Nazi military papers. *(Courtesy of AP Images/Susanna Loof)*

according to Arnold, so were many other parents in that time and place. "My hair was pulled," he said while describing his upbringing. "I was hit with belts. So was the kid next door. It was just the way it was. Many of the children I've seen were broken by their parents, which was the German-Austrian mentality. They didn't want to create an individual."

During World War II, Gustav had joined the Nazi party and served in the German army. He served with a military police unit and reached the rank of master sergeant. Gustav left the army in 1943 after he was wounded in action. The wounds that he suffered were both physical and mental. Arnold believes that's why his father became such an extreme disciplinarian.

"I think that being a disciplinarian, being a military guy, made my father more intense in some ways, more into the disciplinarian thing," Arnold said later. "But with the punishments, the next day he would shower you with gifts. He was a very generous guy. . . . But he still had that side of being a soldier in the Second World War, with all the wounds, with all the shrapnel still in his legs and body. He was in tremendous pain a lot of times. He drank because of that."

Going to the movies gave Arnold a temporary escape from his father. When Gustav would forbid Arnold from seeing a certain movie, Arnold rebelled against him. He would sneak into the movie theater by walking in backwards while the audience was walking out.

In spite of his conflicts with his father, Arnold credits Gustav with getting him involved in sports, which led to his involvement with body building. At the age of ten, Arnold began playing soccer. But after three years, he tired of playing a team sport. He wanted to find something where he would be rewarded and recognized for individual achievements: "by the time I was thirteen team sports no longer satisfied me," he writes in his autobiography. "I disliked when we won a game and I didn't get personal recognition. The only time that I really felt rewarded was when I was singled out as being best."

Arnold dabbled in running, boxing, swimming, and throwing the javelin and shot put. He did well in all of those activities, but he still felt unfulfilled. He continued to play soccer, and when his soccer coach decided that lifting weights would be a good conditioning exercise, it caused a dramatic change in his life.

The first time Arnold lifted weights, he found the gratification that was missing in all the other sports that he had tried. "I'm not exactly sure why I chose body building, except that I loved it. I loved it from the first moment that my fingers closed around a barbell and I felt the challenge and exhilaration of hoisting the heavy steel plates over my head."

Along with the satisfaction of meeting and defeating a challenge, Arnold was awed by the rippling muscles and toned bodies of the men working out at the gym. "I had never seen anyone lifting weights before. Those guys were huge and brutal. I found myself walking around them, staring at muscles I couldn't even name, muscles I'd never even seen before. The weight lifters shone with sweat. They were powerful looking, Herculean."

Arnold became fascinated with one body builder, Reg Park. When Arnold was fourteen, he saw Park on the cover of a body-building magazine displayed in a store window.

After winning the Mr. Universe title, Park had a brief movie career playing Hercules in low-budget action movies. Arnold saw his movies many times and was an avid fan of the body builder turned actor. He was eager to read and learn more about him. What he read gave Arnold both a role model and a blueprint for his future. He recalled:

> I scraped up the pfennigs I had left and bought that magazine. It turned out that Hercules was an English guy who'd won the Mr. Universe title in body building and parlayed it into a movie career and then took the money and built a gym empire. Bingo!

I had my role model! If he could do it, I could do it! I'd win Mr. Universe. I'd become a movie star. I'd get rich. One, two, three—bing, bang boom, I found my passion. I got my goal.

Arnold's soccer coach only wanted his players to lift weights for one hour each week. Arnold was so obsessed with body building that he began working out six days a week. Gustav couldn't understand his youngest son's obsession. He asked Arnold: "what will you do with all those muscles once you've got them?"

Arnold explained his plan. After becoming the best built man in the world, he would go to the United States and become an actor. Gustav had wanted Arnold to become a policeman. His mother wanted him to become a carpenter. Gustav believed that Arnold had had some form of mental illness.

"He (Gustav) was genuinely worried about me," Arnold wrote. "He felt I wasn't normal and of course he was right. With my desire and my drive, I definitely wasn't normal. Normal people can be happy with a regular life. I was different. I felt that there was more to life than just plodding through an average existence."

Arnold's obsessive workouts caught the attention of the other body builders. They made the eager, energetic teen their protégé. They taught him exercises to give him flexibility as well as muscularity—chin-ups, sit-ups, leg raises, squats and twists. They came to replace Gustav as a mentor and father figure for Arnold.

"Each of them became a father image for me," Arnold recalled. "I listened less to my own father. These weight lifters were my new heroes. I was in awe of them, of their

size, of the control they had over their bodies."

Arnold's association with the older body builders also introduced him into the world of steroids. Steroids are man-made chemicals that can be used to build muscle and increase strength. Today, the long-term effects from using steroids are well known and documented. Professional and amateur athletes are routinely tested for steroids and if steroids are detected they are banned from most sports.

When Arnold began body building, steroids were widely used and accepted by body builders. They were considered a benign drug that was vital in developing muscle tissue and in giving body builders a competitive edge. Kurt Marnul, who was the reigning Mr. Austria when Arnold began body building, introduced Arnold to steroids.

According to Marnul, when steroids were legal in the 1960s, all the serious weightlifters and body builders used them. "There was no weightlifter in the world that did not take them," Marnul claimed. "You could get prescriptions for them from the doctor. Arnold, never took them, though, without my supervision."

Arnold took steroids both orally and by injection. According to one unnamed body builder, there were times when Arnold took massive doses of steroids. "Arnold took steroids in doses that terrified the other body builders. I saw him swallow eight or nine Dianabols at a time," the body builder claimed.

It's not clear exactly when Arnold quit using steroids. As late as 1974, he was defending his steroid use. In an interview with Barbara Walters he said: "I take steroids because they help me an extra five percent. I do it under a doctor's supervision. The steroids are mild and I do not know an intelligent builder who has been hurt by them."

By 2000, however, Arnold was speaking out against steroid use. On his Web site he stated: "Because of the health risk that's been proven they present, I strongly feel that there is no place for them in body building or any other sport, especially among competitive professionals . . ."

Even without the benefit of steroids, Arnold would have probably excelled at his chosen sport. His attitude, will, and work ethic set him apart from the other body builders. The saying: "no pain, no gain" isn't a cliché to serious body builders. It's more like a way of life. When Arnold worked out, pain wasn't a form of punishment; it was proof that he was doing things correctly.

"When Arnold did squats, sometimes he would faint," recalled Arnold's longtime friend, Albert Busek. "He didn't know his limit. He knew his limit when he fainted. But without fainting, he didn't know his limits."

Gustav became so concerned with his son's obsession that he limited Arnold to three gym visits a week. Arnold got around that restriction by building a home gym. His make-shift gym was set up in his parent's unheated basement. Arnold would workout even when the temperature outside fell below zero.

On the three nights a week when he was allowed to go to the gym, Arnold walked or biked eight miles before working out. To Arnold, the journey wasn't an inconvenience. It was just additional exercise to supplement his usual workout. "I didn't really mind the eight miles," Arnold writes. "I knew it was helping my body, increasing the strength of my legs and my lungs."

When it came to evaluating his progress and critiquing his body, Arnold was his harshest critic. He pinpointed what muscles were the slowest to develop and improve. Then he totally focused on developing them: "there were some muscles that seemed stubborn. They refused to grow as rapidly as the others. I wrote them on note cards and stuck the cards around my mirror where I couldn't avoid seeing them."

By focusing on the slowly developing muscles and areas such as the triceps, legs, shoulders and back, Arnold gradually transformed his body; when he began his serious workouts, he was six feet tall and he weighed around one-hundred-and-fifty pounds. Within six years, he was six-foot two and he weighed two-hundred-and-fifty.

At that time, Austrian men were required to do one year of military service. Arnold was happy and proud to serve his country. Serving in the army wasn't a drastic change to his disciplined lifestyle.

"For me the army was a good experience. I liked the regimentation, the firm, rigid structure. The whole idea of uniforms and medals appealed to me. Discipline was not a new thing to me—you can't do body building successfully without it."

But when it came to obeying orders or chasing his dreams, Arnold chose the latter. While he was still in basic training, Arnold received an invitation to compete in the junior division of the Mr. Europe contest in Stuttgart, Germany. During basic training Arnold and the other recent inductees were under strict orders to stay on the Army base for six weeks. Arnold decided that he would compete and worry about the consequences later.

Arnold had just enough money for a third-class train ticket to Stuttgart. After scaling the wall around the army compound he spent about a day riding the train. When he arrived at the competition, Arnold had to borrow posing trunks and body oil from the other body builders.

Arnold entered the contest with little idea of how to pose and flex for the judges. He remembered the stances and poses of his hero Reg Park in magazine photos. He emulated Park's poses and won the title of Mr. Europe Junior. It was the first of fifteen body-building titles that Arnold would win. The adulation and attention Arnold received made him feel that he was destined for far greater things. "I loved the sudden attention. I strutted and flexed. I knew for certain that I was on my way to becoming the world's greatest body builder."

He got an impressive looking trophy, but there was no cash prize. Arnold had to borrow money to return to basic training. During the competition he met two people who would have a big influence on his career as a body builder. Arnold's new friends lent him the money to return to his army base.

The first new friend, Albert Busek, worked for Rolf Putziger, who owned a gym in Munich, Germany. Putziger was also a publisher of body-building magazines. Busek talked Putziger into offering Arnold a job as a trainer in his gym. "I was interested in Arnold as a great athlete to bring back to Munich," Busek recalled. "I talked to Arnold about it."

The second new friend, Franco Columbu, won the European power-lifting championship the same day Arnold won the Mr. Europe Junior title. They began chatting during the awards ceremony and established a very quick rapport. Both Columbu and Arnold were ambitious and optimistic young men who came from humble origins. Columbu was born in Sardinia

While competing in the Mr. Europe contest, Schwarzenegger met and became fast friends with Franco Columbu, seen here escorting Caroline Kennedy while serving as best man at Schwarzenegger's wedding. *(Courtesy of AP Images/Mike Kullen)*

where his father eked out a living as itinerant peddler selling beans and potatoes.

Arnold tried to sneak back into his army base, but he was caught climbing back over the wall. He was imprisoned for a week, yet it didn't seem to bother him. "I sat in jail for seven days with only a blanket on a cold stone bench and almost no food," Schwarzenegger recalled. "But I had my trophy and I didn't care if they locked me up for a whole year; it had been worth it."

By the time Arnold was released the entire base knew about his body-building title. He was given two days leave and extra time off to work out. A gym was set up for him and Arnold began a regimen of six-hour workouts. As an added perk, he was allowed unlimited quantities of army food. He bulked up by eating four or five meals a day. He added twenty-five pounds of muscle to his already imposing physique.

Shortly after completing his year of military service, Arnold returned to Thal to briefly visit his parents. There was a job waiting for him in Munich, and Arnold was eager to leave his small village. After saying his goodbyes, Arnold boarded a train confidently vowing that he was leaving home for good.

"I knew when I left home that I would never go back except as a visitor," Arnold remembered later. "I looked back and knew, it wasn't home anymore."

three
Mr. Universe

When he arrived in Munich, Arnold Schwarzenegger was dazzled by the vastness and vibrancy of the strange new city. It was truly a world apart from the quiet and quaint Austrian village that had once been his home. Schwarzenegger was alternately awed and energized by his new surroundings. "Munich was ideal for me," he recalled. "It was exciting, one of the fastest cities in middle Europe. Everything there seemed to be happening at once. . . . Even before I was settled and secure, I could see a future for myself. I could grow and expand. For the first time, I felt I could really breathe."

Within just a few days, Schwarzenegger had a serious falling out with his new boss. To his dismay, he found that Rolf Putziger wanted, and expected, to have a sexual relationship with him. Schwarzenegger had been staying as a houseguest of Putziger's for three or four days and slept on a couch before his host suggested that they should share the same bed.

Munich was an ideal setting for Schwarzenegger and his ambitious plans.

Schwarzenegger flatly refused and packed his clothes and left the house. Putziger followed him outside and tried to persuade him to stay. According to Schwarzenegger, Putziger offered him everything he had yearned for. He told Schwarzenegger that it was something that other body builders had done to advance their careers.

"Think about it, Arnold," Putziger asked. "You wouldn't be the first one."

Putziger reminded Schwarzenegger that two body builders who had lived with him now had their own gyms. They were financially secure and Schwarzenegger could enjoy that kind of life. After Schwarzenegger rebuffed him with a firm no, Putziger persisted by telling him that he could make all of his dreams come true. "You know I can get you into films," he said. "I can finance you while you train for Mr. Universe.

Later, I'll send you to America, to California, to train with the big champions."

Schwarzenegger had been tempted by the offer, but he still refused. He didn't care if it cost him his job. He had never wanted to take the easy route to success and fame and he wasn't going to change. Thanks to an intervention by his friend, Albert Busek, Schwarzenegger was able to keep his job. He moved out of Putziger's house and began sleeping in a small storage room at the gym.

After a few weeks, Schwarzenegger saved enough money to rent a spare bedroom in a modest apartment. He shared the bathroom and ate his meals with his landlord. He eked out a living as a personal trainer to the clients at Putziger's gym. In his spare time, he trained and focused on entering the upcoming Mr. Universe competition in London. "At that point my own thinking was tuned in to only one thing: becoming Mr. Universe. In my own mind, I was Mr. Universe; I had this absolutely clear vision of myself up on the dais with the trophy. It was only a matter of time before the whole world would be able to see it too. And it made no difference to me how much I had to struggle to get there."

Schwarzenegger realized that his meager salary as a personal trainer wasn't going to get him from Munich to London. He had no close friends in Munich to lend him money for airfare and lodging, and he was too proud and independent to ask his parents for money.

Reinhart Smolana, who also owned a gym in Munich, became Schwarzenegger's benefactor. One evening, Schwarzenegger waited outside of Smolana's house until the gym owner and body builder returned home. Smolana had competed in the 1965 Mr. Universe competition and had won the title for his height class. Schwarzenegger persuaded Smolana to help him. Smolana called on his friends and took up a collection to send Schwarzenegger to London. After about a month, he raised enough money.

Schwarzenegger's trip to London was the first time that he had ever flown. He didn't speak English, but he had carefully rehearsed the phrase: "I would like to go to the Royal Hotel please." In his autobiography, he claims that when he arrived, he was overwhelmed by the reception he received. According to him, a crowd of about fifty body builders was standing outside of the hotel. They swarmed around Schwarzenegger grabbing and groping his arms while chattering in languages unfamiliar to the visiting Austrian.

"Apparently, they had all been waiting for me. They had heard that I was the first body builder in Europe with 20-inch arms. In America, that measurement wasn't unusual, but in Europe it was phenomenal—especially on someone barely nineteen years old."

Schwarzenegger biographer Laurence Leamer has debunked that story as part of the hype that has surrounded Schwarzenegger's career. Whether the story is true or false, the 1966 Mr. Universe competition made the whole body-building world aware of Schwarzenegger.

After he posed for the audience, Schwarzenegger was called back for an encore. In only three minutes, he had made an indelible impression on the 3,000 spectators. His incredible physique had gotten him there, but his powerful personality transfixed and won over the crowd.

"Of course he was young and had all the right measure-ments," recalled contest judge Jimmy Saville. "But that wasn't it. It was his incredible personality. When he came on-stage,

Schwarzenegger flexes in this 1967 photo. *(Courtersy of Hulton Archive/ Getty Images)*

it was like somebody had turned on all the spotlights. He just lit the stage up."

While Schwarzenegger was the people's choice, he wasn't the judge's choice. Chet Yorton, an American body builder, was crowned Mr. Universe 1966. Schwarzenegger came in second. He was disappointed, but he was determined to learn from his failure. He began to analyze why he came in second and what it would it take to wrest the title from

Yorton. "Aside from my lack of finish, I still had some serious weaknesses. I had come to the contest with something good, but not good enough to win. I had a lot of mass, a great rough cut. My weak points were calves and thighs. I needed to work on posing, on diet, and all the finer points of body building."

Competing for the Mr. Universe title brought Schwarzenegger into contact with Wag Bennett, a prominent member of London's community of body builders. Bennett owned a couple of gyms and he had served as a judge during the Mr. Universe contest. He invited Schwarzenegger to stay as a guest in his home. Schwarzenegger, in no hurry to get back to Munich, accepted Bennett's offer.

While Schwarzenegger was staying with him and his family, Bennett arranged for the young body builder to meet his idol, Reg Park. Bennett had once lived and trained with Park. He called Park and told him: "There's a kid from Austria who's a sensation and you're his hero and he idolizes you," Bennett said. "If I put on a show in London, will you come over and guest-star the show with him?"

Park agreed to guest star in Bennett's show. In January of 1967, Schwarzenegger got to meet his idol. He was awestruck and speechless when he first met him. "It was really incredible seeing my idol for the first time," Schwarzenegger remembered. "I recall having this foolish self-conscious smile on my face. I just kept looking at him and smiling—almost like when a girl has a crush on a boy and she doesn't know what to say. . . . I was absolutely speechless. I was afraid to talk."

During their week of touring together, Schwarzenegger got over his shyness and awkwardness. They trained together and had long discussions about body building. Schwarzenegger displayed an insatiable curiosity and his idol turned mentor patiently answered all of his questions. "I'm sure that I wore him out during the tour," Schwarzenegger admitted. "I collected advice from Reg the whole time. I wrote it all down to take back to Munich and use as it seemed to serve me best."

Before they parted, Schwarzenegger got Park to promise him that he would invite him to his home in South Africa if he won the upcoming Mr. Universe competition. Schwarzenegger didn't really need any additional motivation, but Park's promise gave him an additional incentive to win.

As he expected, Schwarzenegger won the Mr. Universe title in 1967. At age twenty, he was the youngest body builder to win the coveted title. Shortly after his triumph, he contacted Park and reminded him of his promise. Park, a man of his word, arranged for Schwarzenegger to travel to South Africa.

Schwarzenegger stayed with Park and his family for six weeks. During that time they did a barnstorming tour of body-building shows in South Africa. Park was twenty years older, but Schwarzenegger felt comfortable about sharing his unfulfilled dreams and goals with him. He showed Park and his wife, Marion, a handwritten list of what he wanted to accomplish. "I want to win the Mr. Universe many times like Reg," Schwarzenegger proudly announced. "I want to go into films, like Reg. I want to be a billionaire. And then I want to go into politics."

After returning to Munich, Schwarzenegger began planning his next move—to permanently leave Europe and settle in the United States. According to Schwarzenegger biographer Laurence Leamer, a bad business deal hastened Schwarzenegger's decision to come to America. "I got in trouble with the police. Little troubles," Schwarzenegger later said, mysteriously. "I created a situation that forced me to leave. Somebody told me—'Split. Now you have to go to America.'"

.Once again, Schwarzenegger was short of funds for traveling. Fortunately, he found a benefactor in Joe Weider, who had built a business empire around the sport of body building. Weider published body-building magazines, and also sold weights, dietary supplements, and other body-building products through his publications. He also promoted the sport by establishing the International Federation of Body Builders (IFBB).

Schwarzenegger and Joe Weider, creator of the Mr. Olympia body building competition. *(Courtesy of AP Images/Eric Jamison)*

In return for a salary of two hundred dollars a week, a car, and an apartment, Schwarzenegger agreed to promote Weider's products, publications, and competitions. Schwarzenegger also agreed to write articles for Weider's publications. At that time, he didn't have a great command of the English language and probably had help writing the articles.

In late September 1968, Schwarzenegger stepped off of a plane in Miami, Florida. Weider had flown him there to compete in the IFBB's version of the Mr. Universe completion. The two Mr. Universe titles that Schwarzenegger had won in 1967 and 1968 were sponsored by the National Amateur Body Builders Association (NABBA).

Schwarzenegger was confident he would win. His overwhelming self-assurance didn't endear him to his competitors. Fellow body builder Rick Wayne remarked that Schwarzenegger "seemed damned sure of himself. . . . You could tell by his stage manner, his pigeon-toed strut, the way that he carried his enormous chest, that privately he held himself above the other Mr. Universe contestants."

It turns out that Schwarzenegger was both overconfident and overweight. At two-hundred-and-fifty pounds, he was heavier than he should have been for the competition. Schwarzenegger believed that bigger was better, but the judges didn't agree. He came in second to Frank Zane, an American body builder.

That evening Schwarzenegger returned to his hotel and cried himself to sleep. The next day he talked to Weider about his humbling defeat. Weider convinced Schwarzenegger that a move to California would help him to achieve his goals. "I said, 'If you really want to know how the guys train to be champions, why don't I send you to California, and I'll get you a ticket to go there," Weider recalled. "You can become a member [of the gym] there, and I'll set it up for you."

After arriving in Los Angeles, Schwarzenegger moved into a small apartment he shared with another body builder. He gave himself one year to learn the training regimens and techniques of how a champion trains. His plan was to return to Munich to open an office in Germany for Weider and become his European representative.

Schwarzenegger started working out at Gold's Gym in Santa Monica with Zane. The reigning Mr. Universe had also moved to California. They were friendly rivals, but Zane could see that Schwarzenegger was focused on dominating their sport. "Arnold was different," Zane observed. "You could tell the guy had something going on, that he was special. Nothing bothered him. He was totally focused on winning and achieving his goals."

When he wasn't working out, Schwarzenegger worked at getting an education. He took general education classes at Santa Monica Community College and business courses at UCLA. He also worked hard at improving his English, but he wasn't able to lose his accent.

After a year of training, Schwarzenegger trimmed down from 250 to 230 pounds. He won the IFBB Mr. Universe title in 1969, but lost the Mr. Olympia competition to a Cuban body builder, Sergio Oliva. The following year, he took that title from Oliva. It would be the first of Schwarzenegger's seven Mr. Olympia titles.

The same year Schwarzenegger won his first Mr. Olympia title, he made his first movie. By all accounts the 1970 movie, *Hercules in New York*, is terrible. According to James Karen,

A movie poster for Schwarzenegger's first film, *Hercules in New York*
(Courtesy of RAF Industries/Photofest)

who co-starred in the film, Schwarzenegger hated the movie and even tried to buy up the negative.

Schwarzenegger got the role after the movie's two producers, Aubrey Wisberg and Lawrence F. Fabian, contacted Weider and asked for a body builder to star in their film. Weider enthusiastically recommended Schwarzenegger and claimed that he was an experienced actor. "They asked me if he could act," Weider recalled. "I said, Of course he can, in England he was a Shakespearean actor. And they fell for it."

The kindest words written about the film come from Schwarzenegger biographer Laurence Leamer, who writes that Schwarzenegger projected an "immense likability" in the role of Hercules. A more typical review comes from writer and movie critic John Stanley, who writes: "Arthur Allan Seidelman's direction is turgid, Schwarzenegger's voice is horrendously dubbed, and the physical and verbal humor is dreary."

Once *Hercules in New York* was finished, Schwarzenegger's energy and attention returned to body building. From 1970 to 1975, he won six consecutive Mr. Olympia titles. However, some purists still claim that Schwarzenegger resorted to trickery to wrest the title from Oliva, while he insists he was merely emulating former heavyweight boxing champion Muhammad Ali's practice of psyching out an opponent.

During that 1970 Mr. Universe competition it quickly became apparent that Schwarzenegger, the challenger, and Oliva, the champion, would be the two finalists. At the end of the event Schwarzenegger and Oliva did their final round of poses. While the judges pondered the final outcome, the crowd yelled for the two competitors to return for one final pose down. At some point in the final pose down, Schwarzenegger suggested to Oliva that they leave the stage and that Oliva should lead the way. Oliva agreed, but after he walked off Schwarzenegger remained on the stage and continued posing. Many in the audience thought Oliva had quit by walking off. According to Leamer, Schwarzenegger was ahead of Oliva before the final pose down. But the mixture of boos for Oliva and cheers for Schwarzenegger cinched the win. After that defeat, Oliva never won another major body-building title.

That same year, Schwarzenegger also won the titles of Mr. Universe and Mr. World, the triple crown of body building. At the age of twenty-three, Schwarzenegger had achieved his goal of becoming the most famous, and arguably the greatest, body builder of all time.

However, Schwarzenegger's fame and success couldn't protect him from personal tragedies. In 1971, his brother Meinhard died in a car accident. A year later, his father, Gustav, died from a stroke. Schwarzenegger didn't attend either funeral. Focusing on his goals had taken priority over maintaining family ties. Schwarzenegger biographer Nigel Andrews writes that Schwarzenegger wasn't unfeeling, but his behavior "confirms that, then and later in a life of high achievement and tunnel-vision determination, he saw and felt strictly what he allowed himself to see and feel."

After winning his sixth straight Mr. Olympia title in 1975, Schwarzenegger unexpectedly announced his retirement from body building. He was only twenty-eight, but he had accomplished everything in the sport he had set out to do. There was nothing left to prove.

Now he was free to set his sights on achieving his other goals—material wealth, movie stardom, marriage, family, and maybe even success in politics.

four

The Terminator

Schwarzenegger had originally planned to retire from competitive body building a year earlier, after winning the 1974 Mr. Olympia title. But the lure of playing a major role in a body-building film changed his plans.

The film, entitled *Stay Hungry*, was based on a novel by Charles Gaines. Gaines had first met Schwarzenegger in 1972 when he was writing a magazine article about body builders. In Gaines's novel the main character is a body builder named Joe Santo. As Gaines spent more time with Schwarzenegger, he visualized him as the ideal actor to play the role of Santo.

Before Schwarzenegger could be cast in the role of Santo, he and Gaines had to convince Bob Rafelson, the film's director, that Schwarzenegger was right for the part. When Schwarzenegger met Rafelson, he used his considerable charm and powers of persuasion to win him over. "There was a good deal of resistance on his (Rafelson's) part to using Arnold,"

Gaines recalled. "His attitude was 'No way. We are not going to use some know-nothing Austrian body-builder as a main character in a major motion picture.' When I brought Arnold over to Bob's house—Arnold can charm the socks off of a snake—Bob started to see the possibilities."

Rafelson arranged for Schwarzenegger to take acting lessons from Eric Morris, a well-respected acting teacher who had written four books on the craft of acting. Academy Award winning actor Jack Nicholson was one of Morris's best known students. Morris was impressed by Schwarzenegger's intelligence and intuitive talent for acting. "He's a sharp, sharp, sharp guy," Morris said. "He is one of the smartest people that I have ever met. Very few people realize how talented he really is. If he got it into his head that he wanted to become a fine actor, Arnold could do it. He could compete with any of them."

In *Stay Hungry,* the body builder Santo is a former Mr. Austria who comes to Birmingham, Alabama, to compete in a body-building contest. He develops a romantic interest in Sally Field, who plays the manager of the gym where he works out. Jeff Bridges plays a southern gentleman who is competing for Field's affection. Field ends up choosing Bridges over Santo.

Stay Hungry was not a commercial or critical success, but noted film critic Leonard Maltin gave the film a three-star rating and called it an "eccentric mixture of comedy and drama, but many fine scenes: happy performances from Field and Schwarzenegger make it worthwhile." *Newsweek* movie critic, Jack Kroll, called Schwarzenegger "surprisingly good as the muscle man with heart—and pectorals—of gold."

In spite of the weak box office and mixed reviews, *Stay Hungry* gave Schwarzenegger's movie career a boost. For his performance as Joe Santo, he won the 1976 Golden Globe Award for Best New Male Star. It was the only time that Schwarzenegger has won a major acting award.

Schwarzenegger's next film, *Pumping Iron*, was better received and was more of a financial success. *Pumping Iron* was a documentary; Schwarzenegger simply played himself. The film chronicles Schwarzenegger's pursuit of the 1975 Mr. Olympia title. Mugging for the camera and playing himself earned Schwarzenegger some of the best reviews of his brief acting career.

Schwarzenegger poses on the beach for the premiere of *Pumping Iron* at the Cannes Film Festival. *(Courtesy of AP Images)*

In *New York* magazine, critic Nik Cohn wrote: "[Schwarzenegger] lights up the film like neon every time he comes on-screen . . . His physical power is balanced by great humor, prodigious charm . . ."

Although *Pumping Iron* was only Schwarzenegger's fourth film, he had already learned how to get maximum screen time out of each scene. He was also well aware of how to make a lasting impression on the audience. "I knew the more outrageous I was, the more screen time I would get," Schwarzenegger said, "and the more I would be remembered by the audience."

When he wasn't acting, Schwarzenegger pursued business deals and furthered his education. In 1980, he earned a bachelor's degree in business and international economics from the University of Wisconsin in Superior. He completed most of his degree through correspondence classes.

Schwarzenegger was also cashing in on his fame by starting a mail-order business selling fitness books and cassettes. He invested the profits in real estate. Schwarzenegger was probably a millionaire by age thirty. In 1991, *Current Biography Yearbook* reported that he was one of the ten wealthiest entertainers in the United States. Today, his net worth is estimated to be in the hundreds of millions of dollars.

Schwarzenegger's singular pursuit of wealth, fame, and success might have been satisfying for him, but was not so gratifying for the women he was romantically involved with. Schwarzenegger's first serious relationship in the U.S. was with Barbara Outland. They met when she was nineteen and Schwarzenegger was twenty-two. Schwarzenegger and Barbara stayed together for five years before going their separate ways.

During their relationship Barbara had waited for Schwarzenegger to end his obsessive pursuit of body-building fame. When Schwarzenegger switched his focus from body building to acting, Barbara soon realized that he was never going to settle into a life of marriage and children with her. "It's a typical woman thing," Outland said. "You just want your nest. I could have left him at any time, but I didn't want to, until I finally decided I'm never going to get my dream here. I've got to find it."

Schwarzenegger's next romantic relationship was with Sue Moray, a hairdresser in an upscale Beverly Hills salon. They met at Venice Beach in July 1977. Within a few days, they were living together. Schwarzenegger set down the rules of their relationship and she agreed to them.

"When he was in town, he would be committed to me and I would live with him and go to work from his house.," Moray said. "We would both be faithful when were both in L.A., see each other exclusively, and not go out with anyone else. But when he was out of town, we were free to do whatever we wanted and to date anyone else we wanted."

This "open" relationship wasn't destined to last. About a month after meeting Sue, Schwarzenegger met his future wife Maria Shriver. Shriver came from a family that was wealthy, famous, and politically connected. Her mother, Eunice, was a sister of former U.S. president, John F. Kennedy, and current U.S. Senator Edward Kennedy. Maria's father, Sargent, was the first director of the U.S. Peace Corps and was also the Democrat's nominee for vice-president in 1972.

Schwarzenegger and Maria met in Forest Hills, New York while Schwarzenegger was playing in the Robert F. Kennedy Tennis Tournament. The tournament was named after the

Maria's family was affluent and politically connected. Pictured here from left to right are: Bobby, 10; Timothy, 4; Mrs. Eunice Shriver (sister of President John F. Kennedy), who holds four-month-old Mark; Maria, 8; and Sargent Shriver. *(Courtesy of AP Images/B.H.R.)*

younger brother of the former president who had served in the Kennedy Administration as the U.S. Attorney General. He later served in the U.S. Senate, representing New York. Like his brother, Robert's promising political career was abruptly ended by an assassin during his run for the presidency in 1968.

Maria was twenty-one when she met Schwarzenegger. Like Schwarzenegger, she was focused, ambitious, and had a strong desire to be in the public eye. But instead of acting, she sought to become a television journalist.

Schwarzenegger had once said that he was looking for a woman: "that's brighter than I . . . an aggressive woman who can talk and is not always in the background." Maria had those qualities, along with striking physical beauty. Schwarzenegger was accustomed to being around attractive women, but Maria's large green eyes and alluring smile were very compelling. She, in turn, was attracted by Schwarzenegger's self-assurance and ambition. According to Schwarzenegger, she was the first to fall in love. "She always says that the first time she met me she really liked me," Schwarzenegger recalled. "And it was like love at first sight. I'm slower about these things. I don't jump. As time went on, the more I talked to her and the more I saw her, I started to love her."

For about a year, Schwarzenegger continued to see both Sue and Maria. Sue knew about Maria, but Maria didn't know about Sue. Schwarzenegger would tell Sue that Maria

Schwarzenegger dated Maria Shriver for eight years before they were engaged. This 1983 photo shows Shriver with Schwarzenegger as he displays his U.S. citizenship papers. *(Courtesy of AP Images/Wally Fong)*

was merely a friend, but she couldn't believe him. In August 1978, she gave up and left Schwarzenegger.

Schwarzenegger and Maria dated for around eight years before they got engaged. They loved each other, but were both dedicated to pursuing their careers. In August 1985, Schwarzenegger took Maria to his native village of Thal, Austria. During that getaway, he proposed and Maria accepted.

But soon after she returned from Austria, CBS offered Maria the position of co-hosting the *CBS Morning News* with Forrest Sawyer. "I had to make a wrenching decision," Maria told interviewer Nadine Brozan. "It was the job that I'd always wanted. But I had worked a long time at that relationship, and it had just finally gotten where I wanted it, and all of a sudden I was faced with moving 3,000 miles away and pursuing a very demanding job. But I knew that if I didn't take it there were other people who would."

When Maria decided to take the position, Schwarzenegger supported her. He even encouraged her to negotiate for equal air time with Sawyer. They maintained a long-distance relationship by seeing each other on weekends. During their long courtship, Schwarzenegger starred in the films that would largely define his acting career and solidify his position as an internationally famous action hero.

The first of the films was *Conan the Barbarian,* released in 1982. Conan was the creation of Robert E. Howard, a prolific writer of adventure and fantasy stories that were first published in the 1930s, but gained a new audience when Conan became a comic book hero in the 1960s and 1970s.

Schwarzenegger immersed himself in the role of the brawny warrior who is sold into slavery before avenging

In 1982, Schwarzenegger starred as Conan in *Conan the Barbarian.* *(Courtesy of AP Images/HO)*

the death of his parents and righting other wrongs and injustices. He did all of his own stunts—and sustained some injuries during the filming, including being bitten and kicked by a camel, and run over by horses. During a scene where Conan was attacked by wolves, Schwarzenegger fell down and landed on his back and had to get stitches to close up his wounds.

Conan was a huge commercial success, grossing more than $100 million worldwide. It was also unmercifully panned by movie critics. Peter Rainer of the *Los Angeles Herald Examiner* called Schwarzenegger's portrayal of Conan "about as emotive as a tree-trunk." *Newsweek's* movie reviewer trashed Schwarzenegger's acting by unfavorably comparing it to a famous television and movie dog. He called Conan: "a dull clod with a sharp sword, a human collage of pectorals and latissimi who's got less style and wit than Lassie."

A lot of actors would have been devastated by such scathing reviews, but Schwarzenegger was unfazed. He was more concerned with being an entertainer than in being critically acclaimed as a serious actor. "I want to entertain more people

Schwarzenegger's role as an unstoppable android in *The Terminator* earned him some of the best reviews of his movie career. *(Courtesy of Hemdale/Photofest)*

than any actor ever has," Schwarzenegger said. "But I will stay away from serious shows. I want to be part of the entertaining show, make people laugh and have a good time."

In his next movie, *The Terminator*, Schwarzenegger played a twenty-first century android. The memorable role would earn him some of the best reviews of his career. Schwarzenegger plays an android from the year 2029 that is sent back in time to kill a young, pregnant woman. The woman is being targeted because her unborn son will one day lead a revolution to overthrow the robot society that rules the future world.

The film mixes fantasy and horror with well paced suspense and special effects.

Much like Schwarzenegger himself, the *Terminator* is totally relentless and utterly determined in pursuing what he wants. The simple three-word line "I'll be back" soon became one of the most famous and memorable phrases in action movie history because it concisely expressed the single-mindedness of a villain that couldn't be killed.

Time magazine named *The Terminator* one of the ten best films of 1984. Film critic Leonard Maltin praised both Schwarzenegger's acting and the film: "Schwarzenegger is perfectly cast as violence-prone robot that cannot be stopped. Terrific action picture never lets up for a minute—a model for others to follow." Critic John Stanley summed up the movie's appeal by calling it "an incredibly satisfying viewing experience . . . the whole thing is one big success."

Schwarzenegger's next film, *Red Sonja*, is notable because Schwarzenegger was rumored to have had an off-screen affair with his costar Brigitte Nielsen. Nielsen, a statuesque, six-foot-one Danish beauty played the title role as a female version of Conan. Nielsen supposedly told Schwarzenegger: "I want to move to America to be your wife or woman." If they did have a relationship, it was short lived. Nielsen did achieve her goal of coming to the United States and marrying a movie star, however. She later wed Sylvester Stallone, but the marriage lasted less than two years.

At that time, Schwarzenegger and Stallone had more in common than an interest in Nielsen. They were both vying to be the world's most popular action/adventure movie star. Schwarzenegger's next film, *Commando*, had several similarities to Stallone's highly successful 1985 movie, *Rambo*

First Blood Part II. In *Commando*, Schwarzenegger plays a retired army lieutenant-colonel who goes on a killing spree to rescue his kidnapped daughter. The movie was denounced by critics for being excessively violent; more than one hundred deaths are depicted. *Premiere* magazine called the picture the most violent film of all time.

The movie's producer, Joel Silver, acknowledged the similarities between the two films by saying: "Of course, *Rambo* and *Commando* have a lot in common. They are both larger than life stories about cartoon-like characters that take on enormous odds and win. I think, because of Arnold, *Commando* has a sense of humor that *Rambo* doesn't have."

Although *Commando* had a higher death toll than *Rambo*, it didn't have higher numbers at the box office. But it did well enough to bolster Schwarzenegger's reputation as an international movie star.

At the age of thirty-eight, Schwarzenegger certainly looked like a man who had it all—immense wealth, fame, and success in everything he had set out to do. But he was ready to begin a new phase of his life and take on some new roles outside of acting—that of husband, father, and perhaps even aspiring politician.

five
Political Beginnings

On April 26, 1986, Arnold Schwarzenegger decided to end his bachelorhood, marrying Maria Shriver. The wedding, held at the St. Francis Xavier Church in Hyannis, Massachusetts, was a star-studded gala. Among the five hundred guests were Maria's friends from television—Oprah Winfrey, Diane Sawyer, Tom Brokaw, and Barbara Walters. Former first lady Jacqueline Onassis and Maria's uncle, Senator Edward Kennedy, were also in attendance. Schwarzenegger's longtime friend, Franco Columbu, served as his best man.

After taking their wedding vows, the couple moved into a lavish $4-million house in Pacific Palisades, California. Maria continued to work in New York and Schwarzenegger continued to support her television career. They worked to maintain their long-distance relationship. "We fly back and forth as much as possible and run up thousands of dollars in phone bills," Schwarzenegger told an interviewer.

Schwarzenegger and Maria on their wedding day *(Courtesy of AP Images/ David Tenenbaum)*

With the birth of four children between 1989 and 1997, Schwarzenegger and Maria became more focused on their family. They still pursued their careers, but Schwarzenegger began to want to become more than a celebrity actor and entertainer. Maria's father, Sargent Shriver, encouraged Schwarzenegger to do more outside of acting. "You're an expert on health and fitness, Sargent would tell me. So why don't you continue your education and work in that area. I remember him just pushing me and pushing me."

The time that he was spending with his father-in-law increased Schwarzenegger's interest in politics. Sargent had years of experience being close to the center of political power

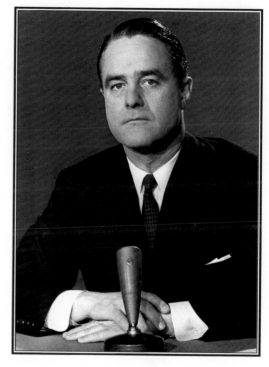

Maria's father, Sargent, encouraged Schwarzenegger to pursue a career in politics. *(Courtesy of AP Images)*

and Schwarzenegger would ask him countless questions and absorb his answers. "I would sit there for hours and just pump him for information," Schwarzenegger said, "because I think that this is a rare opportunity to talk to someone who has worked with the Kennedy Administration, the Johnson Administration and the Nixon Administration."

In spite of his growing interest in politics, Schwarzenegger waited until 1988 to become actively involved in a political campaign. From 1986 to 1988 he starred in five movies. Four of the five—*Raw Deal, Predator, The Running Man,* and *Red Heat*—could be classified as action/adventure films with plenty of violence and killings. *The Running Man* differed slightly from the others in its futuristic setting in the year 2019.

When he was asked about the excesses of violence and killings in his film roles, Schwarzenegger joked about it by saying: "I have a love interest in every one of my films—a gun." He further defended the use of violence by saying that his characters were merely acting in self defense. "My characters just defend themselves," Schwarzenegger told an interviewer. "The message that is sent is to be strong and to be smart and to rely on yourself to get out of danger, to save your own life."

In the 1988 comedy film, *Twins*, Schwarzenegger broke away from playing the avenging action/adventure hero, the sort of roles that were beginning to typecast him. He so wanted to break out of the action mold that he agreed to work without a flat fee and to instead be paid a percentage of the film's total gross receipts. He reportedly received 17.5 percent of the film's $110 million gross, eventually amounting to more than $19 million of the domestic gross. *Twins* also grossed an additional $104.7 million internationally. Schwarzenegger got a smaller percentage of the international gross, but it still amounted to additional millions for him. Soon, other major movie stars such as Bill Murray, Harrison Ford, and Jack Nicholson were negotiating similar deals.

In *Twins,* Schwarzenegger played a character named Julius Benedict, who was the product of some far fetched genetic breeding. Scientists had tried to create the perfect human being by blending the sperm of six highly intelligent men. Then, the sperm is used to impregnate a gorgeous young woman. The unexpected result is the birth of the genetically superior Julius and a physically and ethically inferior brother, Vincent, who is played by Danny DeVito.

After being separated at birth, the "twins" discover each other when they are thirty-five years old. The image of Schwarzenegger as an impish, naïve bumpkin dressed in high-top tennis shoes, baggy shorts, and a thigh-length sports coat contrasted memorably with Devito's diminutive, pony tailed, streetwise con man. Critic Leonard Maltin noted how well the two stars played off of each other: "Effectively blends sentiment and roughhouse humor, with the two mismatched stars packing extra punch in their delightful performances."

Before making his next movie, Schwarzenegger made his first foray into politics. In 1988, George H. W. Bush was the Republican presidential nominee. Bush had served two terms as President Ronald Reagan's vice-president. Schwarzenegger attended the Republican National Convention when Bush was nominated.

Since becoming a United States citizen in 1983, Schwarzenegger had supported Republican candidates. He had been an admirer of President Reagan and wanted Bush to succeed him. He helped to raise money for the Republicans and also introduced Vice-President Bush at a campaign rally in Columbus, Ohio.

After Bush was elected president, he rewarded Schwarzenegger by appointing him chairman of the President's

Schwarzenegger helped raise funds for the Republican party and supported George H. W. Bush during his campaign for president. *(Courtesy of AP Images/Charles Bennett)*

Council on Physical Fitness and Sports. Schwarzenegger enthusiastically used the position to urge Americans to become more physically active. He used his own funds and private jet to visit all fifty states. Schwarzenegger met with the governors of all but one state. Bill Clinton, who was then serving as governor of Arkansas, declined to meet with Schwarzenegger.

Schwarzenegger's chairmanship was a useful introduction to politics for him. It was like running for office without making speeches or asking for votes. It enabled him to network with prominent politicians while keeping himself in the public eye.

Before taking on the position in the administration of the first President Bush, Schwarzenegger had been actively engaged in charities that promoted athletic competition and physical fitness. In the late 1960s, Schwarzenegger's mother-in-law, Eunice Shriver, founded the Special Olympics. The annual event gave mentally impaired athletes an opportunity to

Schwarzenegger trains Special Olympians. *(Courtesy of AP Images/Marty Lederhandler)*

compete against each other. In the late 1970s, Schwarzenegger became the national weight-lifting coach for the Special Olympics. He generously donated his time to coach the athletes and to contact foreign leaders to arrange host countries for the annual event.

Along with his work for the Special Olympics, Schwarzenegger also served as the executive commissioner and as a major fundraiser for the Inner-City Games. That event began in 1991 to give underprivileged children in the Los Angeles area opportunities to compete in sports as well as cultural and educational programs. Thanks to Schwarzenegger's leadership and fundraising, the Inner-City Games expanded to include other cities. Schwarzenegger and the games founder, Danny Hernandez, used Arnold's private jet to set up Inner-City Games throughout the U.S.

In spite of all his charitable works, Schwarzenegger was still dogged by questions about his past. He knew that if he continued to pursue a political career, his father's Nazi background would be closely scrutinized. He decided the best way to deal with it was to be proactive rather than reactive. Since the mid-1980s Schwarzenegger had been a generous benefactor of the Simon Wiesenthal Center and its founder, Rabbi Marvin Hier. Hier had founded the Simon Wiesenthal Center in Los Angeles to preserve the memory of the Nazi Holocaust in World War II. During the Holocaust 6 million Jews perished at the hands of their Nazi captors. Simon Wiesenthal was a Holocaust survivor who dedicated his life to hunting down and capturing Nazi war criminals.

According to Hier, Schwarzenegger called him and said: "Look, I'm in sort of a difficult situation. I'd like to know what my father did during the Second World War."

The exact nature of Gustav's involvement and role with the Nazi's had never been discussed within the Schwarzenegger family. Schwarzenegger knew that there were plenty of rumors about Gustav's involvement in the Nazi Party. He wanted to learn the truth.

A few weeks later, Hier called Schwarzenegger with the results of his investigation. The Center had located a card identifying Gustav as a party member, but they had found no evidence that Gustav had committed war crimes. Schwarzenegger was relieved by the news, but questions about Gustav's Nazi past would resurface years later when he ran for governor.

During his tenure as the Chairman of the President's Council on Physical Fitness and Sports, Schwarzenegger still found time to star in four more movies. The 1990 film, *Total Recall*, was the first of the four. Based on a short story by noted science fiction writer, Phillip K. Dick, *Total Recall* cast Schwarzenegger as a construction worker in the year 2084 who discovers that his boring, uneventful life is a cover for his previous life as a spy.

Total Recall has the most complex plot of Schwarzenegger's films. He described the movie as "strange and bizarre" and "as much about the nature of reality and dreams as it is an action film." Movie critic and science fiction film buff C.J. Henderson described the film's complexity: "The story is laid out with extreme intricacy. Indeed, it takes most folks at least two viewings to decide once and for all whether or not Schwarzenegger is a hero or an idiot. The film offers no clear-cut answer, intelligently leaving the ending totally up in the air."

Having to see a movie twice to really understand it was good for the box office. *Total Recall* earned blockbuster status by grossing over $119 million in the U.S.A. and an additional $142 million in the overseas movie markets.

Schwarzenegger's next film, *Kindergarten Cop*, was much easier to understand. He plays a police detective who goes undercover as a kindergarten teacher. The film got mixed reviews. The Web site *Rotten Tomatoes* gives it 46 percent favorable and 54 percent unfavorable reviews. One of the main criticisms was the story's lack of continuity. *Kindergarten Cop* goes from being a cop thriller, to a children's comedy, then to a love story before becoming a sentimental story about belonging, before reverting back to a cop thriller.

Despite the so-so reviews, *Kindergarten Cop* grossed over $200 million. In Hollywood, a commercial success is always preferable to an artistic one and *Kindergarten Cop* reinforced Schwarzenegger's stature as a box office draw and as a comedic actor.

The huge success of *The Terminator* made a sequel inevitable. In *Terminator 2: Judgment Day*, Schwarzenegger reprised the role of an android, but this time it's a good guy android sent to protect humanity's future savior from being killed by a rival terminator.

Terminator 2: Judgment Day was a big-budget blockbuster. It cost over $100 million to produce, but its worldwide gross exceeded $500 million. It won Academy Awards for Best Visual Effects, Best Sound Effects Editing, Makeup, and Sound. Schwarzenegger's portrayal of the protector cyborg earned him an MTV Movie Award for Best Male Performer.

While Schwarzenegger was enjoying immense success and adulation, his political benefactor, President George H. W. Bush wasn't faring as well. In 1988, Bush had easily defeated his Democratic opponent, Massachusetts governor Michael Dukakis, by carrying forty of fifty states and getting 54 percent of the popular vote. For most of his term, Bush enjoyed favorable approval ratings. The ratings peaked after Bush organized a coalition of nations to drive Saddam Hussein's military forces out of Kuwait. Shortly after the Persian Gulf War ended in 1991, Bush's approval rating climbed to an incredible 89 percent.

But by early 1992, Bush's approval rating had fallen to 29 percent in some polls. A lingering economic recession and Bush's refusal to pursue and depose Saddam Hussein after the conclusion of the Persian Gulf War helped lead to the sharp decline. Still, Bush didn't face any strong opposition from within his party, and as the incumbent president, Bush had no trouble winning the nomination for a second term.

During the general election his Democratic opponent, Arkansas governor Bill Clinton, used the economic recession to win support. Bush responded to Clinton's hammering on the weak economy by attacking Clinton for avoiding military service during the Vietnam War and for participating in anti-war demonstrations when he was a college student. Bush also emphasized his experience in foreign policy and portrayed Clinton as untested and inexperienced in that critical area.

Bush trailed in the polls throughout the campaign. In the campaign's closing days, Bush was able to narrow the gap, but not enough to win a second term. Neither candidate got more than 50 percent of the popular vote because Ross Perot, a wealthy Texas businessman, had entered the race as a third-party candidate and won 19 percent of the popular vote, although he did not carry a single state. Clinton won a solid 370-168 margin in the Electoral College, carrying thirty-two states.

The end of George H. W. Bush's presidency marked the end of Schwarzenegger's tenure as chairman of the President's Council on Physical Fitness and Sports. But it was not the end of his political career.

six

Jingle All the Way

During the eight years Bill Clinton served as president, Schwarzenegger appeared in eight more movies. None would achieve the blockbuster status of *The Terminator*. The first of the eight would become one of Schwarzenegger's worst reviewed and most unpopular films.

The Last Action Hero premiered in 1993. It was hyped as a movie-within-a-movie because in the story a boy gets a magic movie ticket that sends him into the movie he is watching, where he costars with famous action star Jack Carter (played by Schwarzenegger). They play in a make believe world where cars crash and guns fire without anyone getting hurt. *Today* film critic, Gene Shalit, panned the movie on NBC by saying: "It was supposed to be a movie within a movie. Turns out it's a movie without a movie." Leonard Maltin offered a more detailed criticism: "Genuinely bad writing and an overall air of unpleasantness torpedo this film; good action scenes and occasional clever ideas can't save it." It was reported that *The Last Action Hero* lost over $124 million, which would make it one of the biggest flops in movie history.

Schwarzenegger's next film, *True Lies*, fared much better at the box office and became one of the top grossing films of 1994. Schwarzenegger earned some good reviews for his performance as a spy for a super-secret government agency who masquerades as a nerdy computer salesman. The major criticism of the film was that it tried to be something-for-everyone by combining action/adventure with comedy and romance.

The 1994 film, *Junior*, reunited Schwarzenegger with Danny DeVito, this time cast as scientists who discover a miracle drug that induces pregnancy. DeVito tests the drug on Schwarzenegger and the result defies the laws of nature when Schwarzenegger becomes pregnant. Schwarzenegger's performance netted him a Golden Globe nomination for Best Actor in a Comedy or Musical. It may have been a case of an actor rising above the material he's given. Leonard Maltin praised Schwarzenegger's performance, but added that the film offered "precious few laughs after the initial 'joke' is presented."

In 1996, the Republicans nominated Kansas senator Bob Dole to run against the incumbent President Bill Clinton. Dole enjoyed widespread name recognition. He had served as the majority leader in the Senate and had been the party's vice-presidential nominee in 1976. But, at the age of seventy-three, Dole wasn't perceived as an exciting, dynamic candidate.

Clinton had easily won renomination for a second term and was heavily favored to defeat Dole. That may have been why Schwarzenegger took a passive role in the presidential election. After Dole was nominated, Schwarzenegger didn't make any campaign appearances with him or his running mate, Congressman Jack Kemp.

The 1996 presidential election went off as expected. Dole attacked Clinton and his administration over lapses in ethics, but Clinton benefited from low unemployment and inflation and a strong economy. Once again, Ross Perot ran as a third party candidate but he only received around 12 percent of the popular vote. Clinton received 49 percent of the popular vote and a margin of 379-159 in the Electoral College.

About midway through his second term, Clinton was impeached by the House of Representatives. After previous denials, Clinton had admitted in August 1998 that he had an "inappropriate" sexual relationship with a White House intern named Monica Lewinsky. The relationship with Lewinsky was uncovered after Paula Jones, a former Arkansas state employee, filed a sexual harassment suit against Clinton. Clinton tried to conceal his relationship with Lewinsky from Jones's attorneys and denied it under oath in a deposition. Although Jones's suit was dismissed by a judge, the Republicans in Congress decided the president had committed an impeachable offense.

In December of 1999, in a close party-line vote, the House voted to impeach Clinton on one count of perjury and one count of obstruction of justice. They rejected two other impeachment articles. However, the public opinion polls revealed that a large majority of Americans did not support impeaching the president over a sexual relationship and about

Schwarzenegger did not agree with the Republican Party's decision to impeach President Bill Clinton. *(Courtesy of AP Images/Dave Caulkin)*

two months later the Republican-controlled senate acquitted Clinton of the charges.

Although Schwarzenegger was not a supporter of President Clinton, he thought the Republicans had gone too far by trying to impeach him. In a magazine interview he voiced his strong displeasure over the impeachment proceedings. "That was another thing that I will never forgive the Republican Party for," Schwarzenegger said. "We spent one year wasting time because there was a human failure. I was ashamed to call myself a Republican during that period."

In spite of his estrangement from the party's Congressional leadership, Schwarzenegger remained a loyal Republican. By late 2000, he hired a political consultant, George Gorton, to aid him in a possible run for the governorship of California in 2002. Schwarzenegger also hired Bob White, who had served as the chief of staff for former California governor Pete Wilson. When the two new employees met with Schwarzenegger they told him about the perils of politics.

"I urged him to make the race (for governor)," White recalled, "but I said to him and to Maria, 'Look, I have no doubt whatever about your ability as a campaigner. To the contrary, I think that you may have the greatest natural gifts as a campaigner that I have ever seen, but before you make the decision, you need to understand that you're going to be under scrutiny of a kind that you've never seen before."

What they were telling Schwarzenegger was that anything negative in his past—his father's Nazi background, his use of steroids as a body builder, stories of sexual misconduct on movie sets—would be thoroughly examined, researched, and probably used against him by his political opponents.

Schwarzenegger pondered their advice and deferred a decision on running for office. In the meantime, he turned his attention to promoting his latest movie. Since *Junior* was released, Schwarzenegger had starred in three more films— *Eraser, Jingle All the Way* and *Batman and Robin.*

Eraser offered nothing new for Schwarzenegger's fans. It was the standard action/adventure tale that Schwarzenegger was noted for. It had an abundance of violence and special effects, and was one of the top movie hits in the summer of 1996.

Jingle All the Way was a seasonal Christmas comedy that received mostly negative reviews. Schwarzenegger played an overworked salesman who forgot his promise to buy his son a very popular action figure toy for Christmas.

Schwarzenegger poses with a prop during a promotion for *Eraser*. *(Courtesy of AP Images/Jan Bauer)*

On Christmas Eve, he remembers his promise and then goes into a frenzied search for the sold-out toy. The *Rotten Tomatoes* Web site gives it an overwhelming 84 percent negative review.

For playing the villain, Mr. Freeze, in *Batman and Robin*, Schwarzenegger received $25 million for six weeks work. Once again, Schwarzenegger was in a film that was panned by the critics but was popular with moviegoers. *Batman and Robin* enjoyed a worldwide gross of more than $237 million.

Following *Batman and Robin*, Schwarzenegger didn't make another movie for two years. Then, in 1999, he starred in *End of Days*. Both the movie and Schwarzenegger's portrayal of an alcoholic, ex-cop were uniformly disparaged by film critics. In the movie, Schwarzenegger battles the devil to stop him from impregnating his preordained wife. If the devil succeeds, his wife will give birth to the antichrist. Instead of using brawn or bullets, Schwarzenegger defeats the devil by using his innate goodness.

On the most scathing reviews came from critic Mark Kermode in *Sight & Sound* magazine. Kermode called the film, "Idiotic beyond the point of redemption" and "sinfully stupid." Then for good measure, Kermode attacked Schwarzenegger's performance, writing: "*End of Days* is dreadful enough to make most viewers consider gouging out their eyes to avoid seeing a second time the spectacle of the world's most wooden actor pretending to undergo a spiritual crisis."

Although he was less harsh, John Stanley called Schwarzenegger's performance: "a terrible case of miscasting." One of the few positive reviews came from Ted Anthony of the Associated Press, who called the movie "reasonably entertaining."

Yet, Schwarzenegger's name on a movie marquee was still enough to make the movie a financial success. *End of Days* had a disappointing gross in America, but its popularity with foreign audiences made it a moneymaker.

After making *End of Days*, Schwarzenegger followed one bad film with another. *The 6th Day* has been called Schwarzenegger's worst failure as a major star. The film, released in 2000, reportedly cost $80 million to produce and it only grossed $34.5 million in the U.S. market.

While Schwarzenegger was pondering a run for the governorship in 2002, he sat out another presidential election. In 2000, Texas governor, George W. Bush, defeated Vice-president Al Gore in closely contested and controversial election. Gore won the popular vote, but lost the Electoral College vote after the U.S. Supreme Court ruled that Bush had carried Florida by 537 votes. Florida's 27 electoral votes gave Bush a 271-266 victory in the Electoral College.

Although Schwarzenegger was a supporter of George H. W. Bush, he was more muted in his support of his son, George W. Bush. He may have realized that it was going to be a close election and he didn't want to jeopardize his political future by backing a possible loser.

Schwarzenegger found a safer way to get involved in the political process. He would wait until the 2002 election and support one of California's statewide initiatives. Since 1911, California has had a method where voters can enact measures without using the state legislature, which is known as an initiative. If a group can get enough registered voters to sign a petition, their proposed measure is placed on the statewide ballot to be voted on in the next statewide election. In California, the number of signatures only has to be equal to 5 percent of the total voters in the last gubernatorial election.

Working with his political consultant, George Gorton, Schwarzenegger came up with a popular initiative known as Proposition 49, which called for California to spend up to $550 million from its general revenue funds for expanding after-school programs. One of the reasons the initiative had wide appeal was because it didn't call for any increase in taxes. The programs would be funded only when the state had sufficient funds. California had a large number of children who had nothing to do after school. Many came home to an empty house because their parents had to work; others would idly roam through shopping malls or wander the streets.

Schwarzenegger donated $1 million to the campaign to pass Proposition 49. He also used his celebrity status and connections to raise several million more. It was like running for office without an opponent. He spoke at colleges,

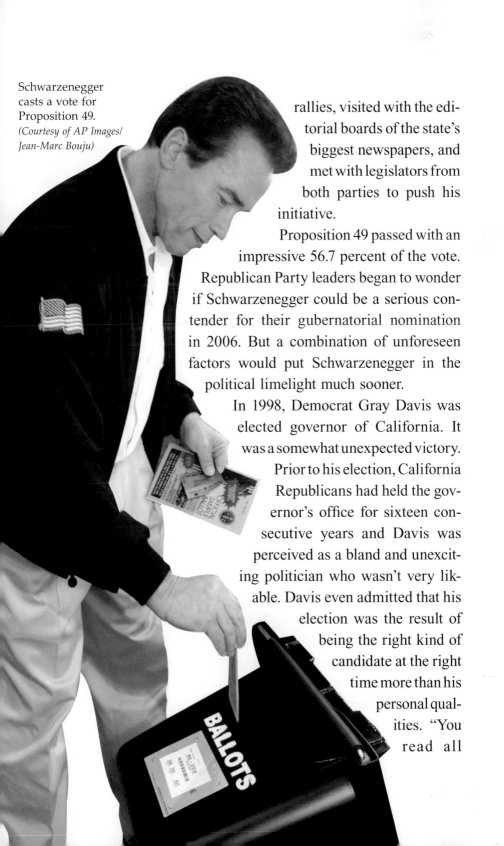

rallies, visited with the editorial boards of the state's biggest newspapers, and met with legislators from both parties to push his initiative.

Proposition 49 passed with an impressive 56.7 percent of the vote. Republican Party leaders began to wonder if Schwarzenegger could be a serious contender for their gubernatorial nomination in 2006. But a combination of unforeseen factors would put Schwarzenegger in the political limelight much sooner.

In 1998, Democrat Gray Davis was elected governor of California. It was a somewhat unexpected victory. Prior to his election, California Republicans had held the governor's office for sixteen consecutive years and Davis was perceived as a bland and unexciting politician who wasn't very likable. Davis even admitted that his election was the result of being the right kind of candidate at the right time more than his personal qualities. "You read all

In 2002, a group of conservatives began a campaign to remove Governor Gray Davis from office. *(Courtesy of AP Images/Paul Sakuma)*

these commentaries about me, and they're always saying how dull and stodgy and predictable, but that's just the way I am," Davis said. "Happily, the people were in the mood for the kind of person that I am."

But by 2002, the mood had changed. Davis was reelected by a narrow margin, even though a poll showed that 60 percent of his fellow Californians had an unfavorable opinion of him. Shortly after Davis's reelection, a group of conservative opponents began a campaign to remove him from office.

In California, an elected official can be removed from office if enough registered voters sign a recall petition. To force a new election, Davis's opponents needed 897,156 registered voters to sign. They exceeded that number by gathering more than 1.3 million certified signatures.

A number of factors contributed to Davis's plummeting popularity. During what was called the dot-com boom, computer companies in California's Silicon Valley made huge profits that led to large tax revenues for the state government. By 2002, the boom was over and there was a multibillion dollar drop in tax revenues.

During the boom years, the state went on a spending spree. Increased spending for education and health care had added another 44,000 employees to the state's payroll. When the slowdown occurred, California's state government found itself facing a $35 billion deficit.

Along with the huge budget deficit, California was in the midst of an energy crisis. In 2001, power outages known as "rolling blackouts" became a common occurrence. Five years earlier, California had enacted laws to deregulate the utility industry. State officials had hoped that the laws would bring about increased competition among electric companies and lower rates for consumers. But by 2000, utility companies were paying increasingly higher prices for electrical power. Because of the new deregulation laws, they couldn't raise their rates and some electrical companies were facing financial ruin. In mid-2001, the state government intervened by buying electrical power for the financially shaky companies.

Davis had also lost popularity because Californians saw him as being too friendly and beholden to certain special interest groups. Practically all politicians take money from and do favors for special interests, but Davis did it in a way that seemed too blatant. Trade unions, Indian tribes with gambling interests, and the California prison guards' union were the main recipients of Davis's favors.

In July 2002, California Lieutenant Governor Cruz Bustamante announced that a recall election would be held on October 7, 2003. The recall would actually be two elections in one. Voters would decide if Governor Davis should stay in office. If they decided to remove him, then they would also vote to decide his successor.

At that time, Schwarzenegger was still uncertain about running for governor. Yet, he was certain of one thing. If he did run, he would campaign with the same zest, energy, and attitude that he showed during body building competitions. He would be in it to win.

seven

Recall

By midsummer of 2003, Schwarzenegger still had reservations about running for governor. One daunting obstacle was getting Maria's approval. When she married him, she believed she would be avoiding a life in politics. One day, while they were lounging in their Jacuzzi, Schwarzenegger told Maria about his political aspirations. The news must have taken her by surprise because she had a physical reaction to it. "We were sitting in the Jacuzzi one day and I said that I wanted to run for Governor—and she started shaking and crying," Schwarzenegger recalled.

It took Maria a few weeks to decide. That upset Schwarzenegger's campaign advisors, but he wasn't going to run without his wife's consent. Maria agreed to support Schwarzenegger after she talked it over with her mother. "It was very tough for her, but her mother—Eunice Kennedy Shriver—was in favor of me running, so she talked to Maria, and she finally agreed," Schwarzenegger said. "If she hadn't agreed, I wouldn't have done it, because my marriage and my family are the most important things."

Even with Maria's consent, Schwarzenegger still had to delay his campaign. He had to promote his latest film, *Terminator 3: Rise of the Machines*. If Schwarzenegger hadn't actively promoted *Terminator 3*, it probably still would have been a big commercial success. But with Schwarzenegger hyping the latest sequel, *Terminator 3* achieved blockbuster status. Its worldwide total gross exceeded $418 million.

Once his promotional duties ended, Schwarzenegger still coyly refrained from announcing his candidacy. According to the polls, there was only one potential opponent who could defeat Schwarzenegger, California's Democratic senator, Dianne Feinstein, who was reading the same polls Schwarzenegger was reading. As a Democrat, she certainly wanted for her party to hold on to the governor's office. But since Schwarzenegger had yet to announce he was running, she didn't feel a need to enter the race.

If Schwarzenegger was interested in making a serious run for governor, time was running out. The filing deadline was mid-August 2003. He was talking to his political consultant, George Gorton, everyday but in early August, even Gorton didn't know Schwarzenegger's plans. After Schwarzenegger joked with him about announcing his candidacy on Jay Leno's *Tonight Show*, Gorton doubted that Schwarzenegger was going to be a serious candidate. "You know, if I were to run, what would you guys think if I were to announce on the Leno show?" Schwarzenegger asked Gorton and his wife, Kiki. They laughed because they thought Schwarzenegger had to be joking.

On August 6th, Senator Feinstein announced that she would not be a candidate for governor. That same day,

Schwarzenegger announced his candidacy for governor of California during an appearance on *The Tonight Show*. *(Courtesy of AP Images/Kevork Djansezian)*

during a taping of *The Tonight Show*, Schwarzenegger teased the host Jay Leno and the studio audience by joking about his possible candidacy. "It is the most difficult decision I've ever made in my entire life, except for the one in 1978 when I decided to get a bikini wax," Schwarzenegger joked.

Schwarzenegger continued to convince Leno and the audience that he wouldn't be a candidate. When he thought they were convinced, he made his surprising announcement. "The man that is failing the people more than anyone is Gray Davis," Schwarzenegger said to Leno. "He is failing them terribly. And this is why he needs to be recalled. And this is why I am going to run for governor of the state of California."

The first television interviews Schwarzenegger did after *The Tonight Show* announcement didn't go well.

On the *Today* show, co-host Matt Lauer twice asked Schwarzenegger if he would make his tax returns public. Both times, Schwarzenegger claimed that he didn't hear the question. Lauer also asked Schwarzenegger that if he were elected, would he repeal California's recently passed paid family leave law. Schwarzenegger was obviously unprepared for the question and he fumbled his way through it. " I-I will have to get into that, I mean, because, as you know, I'm very much for families, I'm very much for children and children's issues and all that stuff."

Later television interviews on *ABC* and *CBS* didn't go much better. The campaign was floundering and his opponents seized the opportunity to characterize him as a political novice and an intellectual lightweight. Maria intervened by shaking up Schwarzenegger's campaign staff. She got Bob White to replace Gorton as Schwarzenegger's campaign manager. "I felt that the campaign needed a massive operation run by someone who had presidential-level experience," she explained. "From the minute that Arnold said he wanted to run, my focus was on putting the best team together to help him do that."

To rebut the charges that he was uninformed on the issues, and unprepared and unqualified to be governor, Schwarzenegger worked hard at getting educated in a short time. For the first two weeks of his campaign, he met with a steady stream of experts on various topics and issues.

Several of Schwarzenegger's advisors thought the process was too time consuming. They felt that the campaign would be better served by Schwarzenegger making speeches and shaking hands. But Schwarzenegger patiently sat through the lectures and by late August he felt confident enough to hold his first press conference.

The first press conference was attended by nearly two hundred journalists. Reporters from American and foreign newspapers, political magazines, tabloid publications, and entertainment magazines were eager to see how well informed and prepared Schwarzenegger was. His opening statement set the tone for both his first press conference and his subsequent campaign.

"When I came to California thirty-five years ago, this was a place of great dreams," Schwarzenegger told journalists. "This state said to the people everywhere, 'Come here. Work hard. Play by the rules and your dreams can come true.'"

Then Schwarzenegger asked a series of rhetorical questions: "What has happened to California? What has happened to that feeling? What has happened to the optimism that this state once represented to the world."

Without answering the questions that he posed, Schwarzenegger presented himself as the candidate who could and would bring those old feelings back.

"Now I believe that we all—in my heart—that we can bring that optimism back. . . . We still have all the elements that made us great and prosperous. We have everything we need, except leadership."

Without going into specifics Schwarzenegger talked about fixing things by calling a special session of the legislature, by improving the business climate to keep jobs from leaving the state, bringing down the cost of energy, and working to reduce the budget deficit.

Schwarzenegger was well aware that he was not presenting many details. He acknowledged that by saying that there weren't any easy answers to California's problems and warned the journalists that it would take some kind of action to fix things. "Before the carping begins about the need for a twenty-five point plan on each of those items, let me make one thing clear: that these problems were not created in two weeks. Nor will we be able to solve these problems in two weeks. Let me tell you something. One thing that the citizens of California can count on is that I would take action."

As soon as the questions began, Schwarzenegger asserted his authority. He told the reporters that if their questions were not asked in an orderly manner, they would go unanswered. No matter what was asked, Schwarzenegger deftly portrayed himself in the most favorable way. Most of the political reporters were frustrated because they couldn't pin him down.

Schwarzenegger answers questions at a press conference. *(Courtesy of AP Images/Kevork Djansezian)*

Schwarzenegger ended the press conference by thanking everyone for coming out and for their prior support. "I want to thank you all for coming, because remember I am a strong believer in that if it was my body building career or my acting career, I could not have done it without the press. You were always very helpful."

The slogan of the campaign was "Join Arnold" After his closing remarks, some reporters felt that Schwarzenegger believed that they had already joined him. But the *Los Angeles Times* was one major newspaper that wasn't about to jump on his bandwagon. The editor, John Carroll, was an old-fashioned journalist who believed that candidates for high office should offer more than glib sound bites and well written speeches. Carroll felt that his paper had a duty to the citizens and voters to learn and report everything they could about Schwarzenegger's character. "We're going to cover his [Schwarzenegger's] character and if the public likes his character as it is, knowing the facts, that's fine," Carroll said. "But no one is ever going to be able to say the *L.A. Times*, when John Carroll was editor, was asleep at the switch and therefore a person with questionable character ascended to high office."

Schwarzenegger had declined Carroll's invitations to meet with him and the members of the *Los Angeles Times* editorial board for a no-holds barred interrogation. Carroll felt that Schwarzenegger was shirking his civic duty as a candidate. Schwarzenegger felt that the meeting would just be a group of experienced, if not hostile, journalists ganging up on a political novice.

Even without a face-to-face meeting, the *Times* got Schwarzenegger to provide detailed answers to their questions. Shortly after Schwarzenegger entered the race, they sent him a

questionnaire asking how he would handle California's financial crisis. Schwarzenegger didn't answer it, so the *Times* ran
a blank space on the page where Schwarzenegger's answers
would have appeared. After that, Schwarzenegger answered
all of their questionnaires.

No amount of questionnaires and thoughtful answers could
quell the rumors and stories about Schwarzenegger exhibit-
ing boorish behavior around women. The *Times* assigned a
task force of reporters to investigate and verify the stories.
Eventually, they would publish an account of Schwarzenegger

Schwarzenegger during his 2003 campaign for governor *(Courtesy of AP
Images/Reed Saxon)*

behaving badly, but would wait until six days before the election to do so.

During his campaign Schwarzenegger had been able to avoid any in-depth interviews with political reporters. The first press conference of his campaign was his only press conference. For the most part, his campaign was a series of staged events with handpicked audiences. He appeared in one debate with the top five candidates. Schwarzenegger, and his four major opponents, had all been given the questions in advance.

Thanks to his advance knowledge of the questions, Schwarzenegger came across as being well-informed on the issues. Gray Davis was sensing that the election was slipping away from him. He summed up Schwarzenegger's huge appeal: "He is arguably the best-known Hollywood celebrity alive," Davis said. "In addition, because of his persona, and

In this photo, Schwarzenegger (far left) is participating in the only televised debate among the top five candidates for governor during the recall vote of 2003. *(Courtesy of AP Images/Rich Pedroncelli)*

the figure that he plays in the *Terminator* movies, he has a very commanding presence. That impacts all his relationships, be it the press, the legislature or with an audience."

Six days before the election, Schwarzenegger's campaign faced its most serious challenge. The *Los Angeles Times* ran a story on page one with the headline: "SIX WOMEN SAY SCHWARZENEGGER GROPED, HUMILIATED THEM." The first sentence of the story reported that all six women said that Schwarzenegger had "touched them in a sexual manner without their consent."

Schwarzenegger's campaign staff had been anticipating the story and was prepared to respond. The staff had already interviewed focus groups to help predict public reaction to a story of that nature. According to those groups, the likely

E. Laine Stockton (left) and Colette Brooks talk about their sexual misconduct allegations against Schwarzenegger. Both claim Schwarzenegger made unwanted sexual advances toward them in the past. *(Courtesy of AP Images/Nick Ut)*

reaction would largely be one of indifference. Stories about movie stars behaving badly and engaging in unseemly behavior were nothing new. Sean Walsh, a campaign staffer, noted that "Most people shrugged [thinking,] 'That's the way things go in Hollywood.'"

Schwarzenegger's campaign manager, Mike Murphy, convinced the candidate that the proper response was to admit that he acted inappropriately, but that such behaviors were commonplace in the movie business. Then, Schwarzenegger would make a blanket apology to anyone that he may have offended. Schwarzenegger was not accustomed to making apologies, especially public ones. But at a campaign rally in San Diego, he started off by saying that most of the allegations were not true. The *Times* story had only named two of the six women accusers. "A lot of those, when you see those stories, it's not true," Schwarzenegger said. "But at the same time, I have to tell you that I always say that wherever there is smoke, there is fire."

Some people in the audience gasped audibly at Schwarzenegger's acknowledgment. Then, he made a combination confession and apology. "And so what I want to say to you is, yes, that I have behaved badly sometimes," Schwarzenegger admitted. "Yes it is true that I was on rowdy movie sets, and I have done things that were not right, which I thought then was playful. But now I have recognized that I have offended people. And to those people that I have offended, I want to say to them, I am deeply sorry about that, and I apologize, because this is not what I am trying to do."

After Schwarzenegger's apology, the *Times* continued to run stories about women saying that Schwarzenegger had groped them. But most voters seemed to be satisfied by his apology. What started out as an investigative journalism piece was now looking more like a vendetta.

On Tuesday, October 8, 2003, Californians turned out in record numbers to decide if they wanted a new governor. It was the largest turnout for a gubernatorial election in more than twenty years. The result was a repudiation of Governor Gray Davis and a resounding victory for Schwarzenegger. On the question of whether Davis should be removed from office, over 55 percent of the electorate voted yes.

On the question of who should replace him, Schwarzenegger led all of the 135 challengers with 48.6 percent of the vote. Schwarzenegger's percentage was more than his two closest rivals—Lieutenant Governor Cruz Bustamante (31.5 percent) and State Senator Tom McClintock (13.5 percent) combined.

Shortly after the election, an article in *Time* magazine summed up how well Schwarzenegger's campaign staff had shielded and sold their candidate: "At a time when other politicians hauled around briefcases full of 100-page platforms, Arnold Schwarzenegger spouted lines from his movies, gave no substantive interviews, and agreed to exactly one debate, for which he knew the questions in advance."

Schwarzenegger might have been a new politician, but he knew that winning the election was the easy part. Now it was time for the hard part—effectively governing America's most populous state.

eight

Governor Schwarzenegger

O n November 17, 2003, Schwarzenegger became California's 38th governor. His transition team tried to downplay the event by officially calling it a swearing-in instead of an inaugural. There were no gala parties or lavish inaugural balls planned. However, Schwarzenegger was too big of a celebrity to keep things completely low-key. There were 7,500 invited guests, more than seven hundred journalists, and a row of 130 cameras broadcast the event all over the world.

In his opening remarks, Schwarzenegger appeared to be genuinely awed that an immigrant from a small Austrian village would be governing 35 million Californians. "I am humbled, I am moved, and I am honored beyond words to be your governor," he said.

Schwarzenegger only spoke for twelve minutes. He vowed to end the partisanship that had plagued the state and to restore confidence in the government. Without mentioning Gray Davis, Schwarzenegger said that the transfer of power was more about changing how the government operated rather than changing governors. "The election was not about replacing one man," Schwarzenegger noted. "It was not about replacing one party. It was about changing the entire political climate of our state."

Following his swearing in, Schwarzenegger quickly got to work. He walked to his office in the Capitol building and signed a bill repealing the recent tripling of California's car tax, a fee that all Californians pay to register their vehicles. Its passage had been one of the things that led to Davis' recall and during his campaign Schwarzenegger had promised to repeal the 300 percent increase.

The car-tax repeal would cost the state treasury an estimated $4 billion in lost revenue. Schwarzenegger proposed making that and other revenue shortfalls up by issuing $15 billion in bonds. He also proposed reducing the state budget by cutting programs and halting the growth of various social services.

State senator Tom McClintock, who had run for governor against Schwarzenegger, became an outspoken critic of the bond proposal. McClintock pointed out that issuing bonds was no different than borrowing on a credit card. Eventually, the money has to be repaid with interest. Traditionally, bonds were not used to fund the state's ongoing expenses.

Despite the criticism, Schwarzenegger made the $15 billion bond issue the cornerstone of his economic recovery program. He also proposed a cap on state spending and to also save by reforming the state's workman's compensation program.

Soon after becoming governor, Schwarzenegger began campaigning for a number of economic propositions designed to bolster California's weak economy. *(Courtesy of AP Images/Damian Dovarganes)*

Schwarzenegger used some deft political maneuvering to bypass legislative opposition to his proposals. He got the Democratic opposition to vote for putting two propositions on the ballot in a special statewide election. Proposition 57 sought approval for the $15 billion bond issue. Proposition 58 would put limits on future government spending. In reality, the two propositions would probably just postpone the state's persistent financial problems. But Schwarzenegger was able to sell the idea that it was the start of a great turnaround. The two measures would be voted on in March 2004.

When Schwarzenegger began campaigning for the measures, only about one-third of the California voters favored them. For him, it was another challenge to be met.

On the campaign trail Schwarzenegger's staff kept him insulated from the media again. He gave few interviews and reporters were usually kept a safe distance away.

In March of 2004, Proposition 57 passed with 63.4 percent of the vote. Proposition 58 received an overwhelming 71.1 favorable vote. It was a strong vote of confidence for a governor who had been in office less than five months.

Schwarzenegger's next triumph was the passage of legislation to reform California's workman's compensation program. When the lawmakers in Sacramento balked at Schwarzenegger's plan, he threatened to take it directly to the voters via another ballot initiative. By mid-April 2004, Schwarzenegger got his bill passed. Even the usually critical *Los Angeles Times* praised the measure by saying the new law was "expected to wring billions of savings from an insurance system often blamed for causing businesses to flee the state."

Trying to balance the state budget while keeping a campaign promise of not raising taxes was Schwarzenegger's biggest challenge. Ultimately, he wasn't able to do both. Making up for a $15 billion budget shortfall was simply too difficult. An estimated $5 billion in temporary spending cuts made up for the vehicle tax shortfall, but that still left a deficit of $10 billion.

Schwarzenegger was able to get the California Teachers Association to give up $2 billion earmarked for educational funding by agreeing that the state wouldn't ask them for any further cuts. He was also able to get additional budget concessions from city and county governments and public universities. By going directly to those groups, Schwarzenegger angered some legislators for not seeking their input.

The final result was a $105 billion budget with a projected deficit of $5 to $7 billion. Daniel Weintraub, a political columnist for the *Sacramento Bee*, opined that Schwarzenegger might have done better, but it was a good start for a political newcomer.

"It would have been nice to see the governor reach higher for the kind of long-term budget reforms that the state dearly needs," Weintraub noted. "But Schwarzenegeer has just taken a chunk out of California's persistent budget shortfall while cutting taxes and building important new political alliances with school leaders, local government officials, university administrators, and freeway builders and labor unions that constitute the transportation lobby. Not a bad start for a novice."

Some economists were less enthused. They saw the budget as just a stopgap measure that put off the inevitable day or reckoning. There were even some projections that the deficit would double in just five years.

In November of 2004, President George W. Bush was reelected to a second term as president. Schwarzenegger had his well-received speech at the 2004 Republican National Convention. Afterward, he campaigned for Bush, but California's fifty-three electoral votes went to the Democratic nominee, Senator John Kerry of Massachusetts. However, Schwarzenegger scored a personal triumph by the approval of some statewide initiatives he had supported.

The most controversial initiative was Proposition 71, which called for California to spend $3 billion on embryonic stem-cell research. Schwarzenegger's support of stem-cell research was in opposition to the Bush Administration's position. The use of embryonic stem cells for medical research is controversial in some quarters because the cells are generated from test-tube embryos and the embryos are destroyed when the stem cells are removed.

Global warming has been another prominent issue where Schwarzenegger has disagreed with most Republicans. Until recently, most prominent Republican leaders have ignored or downplayed the threat caused by the warming of the planet. Cutting against the grain in his party, Schwarzenegger signed a bill called the Global Warming Solutions Act in September 2006. The act requires major industries to reduce greenhouse gas emissions 25 percent by 2020. "The debate is over," Schwarzenegger told newspaper columnist, Thomas Friedman. "I mean, how many more thousands and thousands of scientists do we need to say 'We have done a study that there is global warming?'"

After Schwarzenegger signed the bill, auto manufacturers sued California, claiming that the rigid new standards are illegal. They insist that setting standards for automobiles should be a federal, and not a state matter. Regardless, Schwarzenegger has vowed to enforce the new regulations.

In September 2006, Schwarzenegger signed the Global Warming Solutions Act, which calls for a reduction in the types of greenhouse gas emissions that are responsible for the smog seen in this picture. *(Courtesy of AP Images/Nick Ut)*

"But we will never change back our fuel standards," Schwarzenegger insists. "We will never change back our greenhouse-gas emission standards. The train has left, and if you are going to march forward, the regulations are only going to get tougher, they are not going to get easier."

In the first months after becoming governor, Schwarzenegger had been successful at going over the heads of the Democratic-controlled California legislature by the use of ballot initiatives. However, this strategy of avoiding state senators and representatives did not endear him to legislators from both parties. The increased political controversy began taking a toll on his popularity.

Schwarzenegger's popularity reached a new low in the summer of 2005. Most observers attributed his steep decline to four more ballot initiatives he announced that summer. Because 2005 was not an election year, the initiatives would require a special election. There had been a number of ballot initiatives and elections since the recall of Gray Davis in 2003, and the people of California were growing weary of political commercials, public debate, and having to go to the polls. The once popular initiative system was growing tiresome to many voters.

The ballot initiatives were prompted by the inability of Schwarzenegger and the state legislature to come together on a compromise budget. The state entered the fiscal year that began on June 1, 2005, without a budget. The conflict was over several spending measures. Most critically, the Democrats and Republicans disagreed over spending almost $1 billion on new health care and education programs. The failure to pass a budget meant that millions in payments to schools and other mandated institutions could not be made.

One of the reasons the Democrats and Republican could not get together was the ballot initiatives Schwarzenegger had proposed to be voted on in November. If all four of the initiatives passed there would be a state spending cap, the governor would have the power to make midyear budget cuts without legislative approval, the way legislative districts were drawn would be changed, teachers would have to wait longer to get tenure, and public employees would have their right to contribute to political campaigns limited.

Opponents considered the initiatives to be power grabs on the part of the governor. The teacher unions and organizations were a powerful force in state politics and generally supported Democratic candidates. To limit their tenure would make them more susceptible to being fired. The spending cap would force cuts in popular programs and if the governor could make unilateral budget cuts the Democratic power of the legislature would be severely hobbled. Taking away the legislator's power to carve out districts might have been popular at another time, but it was combined with other measures that seemed to be designed to enhance the power of the executive at the expense of the legislature.

The initiatives were immediately controversial. Teacher unions and public employee unions opposed its passage. Feelings were so high they demonstrated repeatedly and were able to raise thousands of dollars to run commercials and to organize against it. Most Democratic Party leaders were staunchly opposed, as were some Republicans. They suffered another blow when it was announced the special election could cost up to $85 million. It was clearly going to be an uphill battle to win passage for the initiatives.

Schwarzenegger, as was to be expected, campaigned strenuously for passage. As the campaign grew heated he switched from the more moderate, less partisan language and tactics that had served him so well in 2003. He attacked the Democrats in the legislators as being old-fashioned big spenders who wanted to raise taxes and waste money. He and his supporters accused the teachers of being more concerned with their own job security than with education. This type of sharp elbow politics was more similar to the way national campaigns were run and were quite different than what Schwarzenegger had done before.

One of the reasons for the stridency was probably the inability of him and the legislature to reach an agreement.

Schwarzenegger was frustrated and let his frustration color how he campaigned.

The fight over the special election continued to take a toll on Schwarzenegger's popularity. Furthermore, it became increasingly obvious that the initiatives would fail. When the voters went to the polls on November 8, 2005, they rejected the initiatives. Schwarzenegger had suffered a stinging defeat.

Schwarzenegger was down, but he quickly proved he was not out. Two days later he gave a press conference and admitted he had been wrong to call for the initiatives. He also promised to return to the more moderate, less partisan style of governing and campaigning that had served him so well in the past. When one reporter asked him if he would do anything differently, Schwarzenegger joked that "If I was to make another Terminator movie, I would tell Terminator to travel back to tell Schwarzenegger not to have another special election." He went on to promise to operate with "a different mentality" and would try to be more patient when dealing with the legislature.

With a political adroitness that surprised many seasoned political observers, Schwarzenegger immediately began making good on his promise to lower the political tension between him and the legislature. He also set out to repair the damage with teachers and public employees.

There was quite a bit of work to be done to repair his image and many wondered if he would run for reelection in 2006—and if he could win if he ran. His poll numbers were still below 50 percent.

Again, anyone who counted Schwarzenegger out was making a foolish mistake. He steadfastly held to his conviction to hold onto the center. He even went so far as to criticize

Republicans in Washington who he felt were making a mistake by refusing to compromise more with Democrats. He accurately predicted that his party would suffer politically in 2006 across the nation if there was not more flexibility. He called his approach "post-partisanship" and repeatedly said he thought the era of hard-edge partisanship between the major parties was over.

Schwarzenegger's poll numbers steadily improved and he announced he would run for reelection. His standing was also helped by improvement in the California economy, but he also worked harder to discuss the issues that were on the minds of his constituents. One major issue he promised to address if reelected was to find a way to make sure all Californians had health care coverage. He promised to devise a plan that combined what he said were the best parts of both the Republican and Democratic ideas.

The Democrats had a bruising primary that selected state Treasure Phil Angelides as their candidate for governor. Angelides was not a dynamic campaigner. Meanwhile, Schwarzenegger seemed to be improving everyday. Soon it became clear that Schwarzenegger had returned from almost certain defeat; he was leading by a wide margin in the opinion polls. In November 2006, Schwarzenegger was reelected to a second term as governor in a near landslide win. He won nearly 57 percent of the vote.

All was not well, however. About six weeks before the election, the *Los Angeles Daily News* had reported that Schwarzenegger's popularity with Democrats and independents had declined. Among Democrats, his job approval rating fell from 57 to 47 percent from August to September 2004. Among independents, it dropped from 66 to 63 percent.

In November 2006, Democrat Phil Angelides lost to Schwarzenegger in the race for governor. *(Courtesy of AP Images/Paul Sakuma)*

Still, his overall approval rating was 64 percent and among Republicans, it was an impressive 88 percent. His old nemesis, the *Los Angeles Times*, endorsed his reelection by writing: "After his historic election in the 2003 recall, followed by some early promise and a disappointing sophomore year, Arnold Schwarzenegger has been a solid, pragmatic governor who has steered a moderate course for California. He deserves a sequel."

It was clear that he still had to prove that he would continue to try to work to bring the state together to solve problems. The voters had given him another chance, but it was up to him to fulfill his promises. To prove that he intended to do so, Schwarzenegger soon presented his health care reform bill to the California legislature and agreed to work with both sides to forge a strong, affordable plan to ensure universal coverage in California.

Nationally, Schwarzenegger's prediction came true. The Republican Party lost control of both houses of the U.S. Congress. Schwarzenegger began giving national interviews in which he said that more politicians from both parties should take a lesson from his setback in 2005 and learn how to work together. His "post-partisan" approach was the future, he said, and was the only way the country could face problems such as terrorism and global warming.

When his second term ends, Schwarzenegger will be sixty-three years old. Because he wasn't born in the United States, the U.S. Constitution prohibits him from serving as president. In December 2004, the newspaper *USA Today* ran a story asking if the U.S. Constitution should be amended so Schwarzenegger could become president. The answer was a strong "no!" and this doesn't seem likely to change.

Does Schwarzenegger have a political future after his second term ends? A run for the U.S. Senate is a possibility. If a Republican is elected president, a position in the cabinet post is another possibility.

Since Schwarzenegger has spent most of his adult life in the public eye, it's unlikely he will quietly fade from the public view.

Regardless of what he chooses to do, Arnold Schwarzenegger will face the challenge with unyielding perseverance and commitment. As surely as he followed his dream of leaving Austria to become a bodybuilder and movie star, he will follow his political dreams as far as he can.

Timeline

1947   Born July 30 in Thal, Austria.

1965   Wins his first body building contest, Mr.
Europe Junior.

1966   Places second in the Mr. Universe competition.

1967   Wins Mr. Universe for first time.

1968   Moves to the United States.

1970   Wins first of seven Mr. Olympia titles; debuts in film
Hercules in New York.

1975   Announces his retirement from body-building
competitions.

1976   Wins Golden Globe Award for Best New Male
Star in *Stay Hungry.*

1977   Stars in *Pumping Iron*; best-selling autobiography
and body-building manual, *Arnold: The Education
of a Body Builder*, is published.

1980   Comes out of retirement to win the Mr. Olympia
title for the seventh time.

1982   Stars in *Conan the Barbarian.*

1983 Becomes a citizen of the United States.

1984 Stars in *Conan the Destroyer* and *The Terminator.*

1986 Weds Maria Shriver.

1990 Appointed chairman of President's Council on Physical Fitness and Sports.

1991 Stars in *Terminator 2*; establishes the Inner-City Games.

2000 Leads a successful campaign to pass California ballot measure, Proposition 49, which expanded before- and after-school care for children.

2003 Stars in *Terminator 3*; elected governor of California.

2006 Reelected governor of California.

Sources

CHAPTER ONE: My Fellow Americans

p. 12, "My fellow Americans . . ." Laurence Leamer,
Fantastic: The Life of Arnold Schwarzenegger (New
York: St. Martin's Paperbacks, 2005), 7.

p. 12, "I was born in Europe . . ." Ibid.

p. 14, "I want you to know . . ." Ibid, 10.

CHAPTER TWO: Second Son

p. 16, "Ever since I was a child . . ." Daniel Bial,
Arnold Schwarzenegger Man of Action (New York:
Franklin Watts, 1998), 19.

p. 16, "Tell me, which one of you . . ." Wendy Leigh,
Arnold: An Unauthorized Biography (Chicago: Congdon
& Weed, Inc., 1990), 14.

p. 16, "He would correct it . . ." Leamer, *Fantastic: The
Life of Arnold Schwarzenegger*, 17.

p. 17, "My hair was pulled . . ." Ibid., 18.

p. 18, "I think that being a . . ." Ibid., 18-19.

p. 18, "by the time I was thirteen . . ." Arnold Schwarzenegger
and Douglas Kent Hall. Arnold: *The Education of a
Body Builder* (New York: Simon and Schuster, 1977), 14.

p. 19, "I'm not exactly sure . . ." Ibid.,13.

p. 19, "I'd never seen anyone . . ." Schwarzenegger and Hall,
Arnold: The Education of a Body Builder, 14.

p. 19-20, "I scraped up the pfennings . . ." Leamer, *Fantastic:
The Life of Arnold Schwarzenegger*, 25.

p. 20, "what will you do . . ." Ibid., 19.

p. 20, "He was genuinely worried . . ." Ibid.

p. 20-21, "Each of them became . . ." Ibid., 15.

p. 21-22, "There was no weightlifter . . ." Nigel Andrews, *True Myths The Life and Times of Arnold Schwarzenegger* (Secaucus, N.J.: Birch Lane Press, 1996), 22.

p. 22, "Arnold took steroids in doses . . ." Leigh, *Arnold: An Unauthorized Biography*, 27.

p. 22, "I take steroids because . . ." Karen Brandon, *Arnold Schwarzenegger* (San Diego: Lucent Books, 2004), 40.

p. 22, "Because of the health risk . . ." Ibid.

p. 22, ""When Arnold did squats . . ." Leamer, *Fantastic: The Life of Arnold Schwarzenegger*, 52.

p. 23, "I really didn't mind . . ." Schwarzenegger and Hall, *Arnold: The Education of a Body Builder*, 20.

p. 23, "there were some muscles that seemed stubborn," Ibid., 35.

p. 23-24, "For me the army . . ." Ibid., 35-36.

p. 24, "I loved the sudden attention . . ." Ibid., 37.

p. 25, "I was interested in Arnold . . ." Leamer, *Fantastic: The Life of Arnold Schwarzenegger*, 38-39.

p. 26, "I sat in jail . . ." Schwarzenegger and Hall, *Arnold: The Education of a Body Builder*, 37

p. 26, "I knew when I left . . ." Andrews, *True Myths: The Life and Times of Arnold Schwarzenegger*, 28.

CHAPTER THREE: Mr. Universe

p. 27, "Munich was ideal for me . . ." Schwarzenegger and Hall, *Arnold: The Education of a Body Builder*, 41.

p. 28, "Think about it, Arnold . . ." Ibid., 42.

p. 28-29, "You know I can get you into films . . ." Ibid.

p. 29, "At that point my own thinking . . ." Ibid., 43.

p. 30, "I would like to go to . . ." Ibid., 47.

p. 30, "Apparently, they had all been waiting . . ." Ibid.

p. 30-31, "Of course, he was young . . ." Leigh, *Arnold: An Unauthorized Biography*, 55.

p. 32, "Aside from my total lack . . ." Schwarzenegger and Hall, *Arnold: The Education of a Body Builder*, 52.

p. 32, "There's a kid from Austria . . ." Leamer, *Fantastic: The Life of Arnold Schwarzenegger*, 58.

p. 32, "It was really incredible . . ." Schwarzenegger and Hall, *Arnold: The Education of   a Body Builder*, 61.

p. 33, "I'm sure that I wore him out . . ." Ibid., 63.

p. 33, "I want to win the Mr. Universe many times . . ." Leamer, *Fantastic: The Life of Arnold Schwarzenegger*, 66.

p. 34, "I got in trouble . . ." Ibid.

p. 35, "seemed damn sure of himself," Leamer, *Fantastic: The Life of Arnold Schwarzenegger*, 69.

p. 35, "You could tell by his stage manner . . ." Ibid.

p. 35-36, "I said, 'If you want to really . . ." Ibid., 71.

p. 36, "Arnold was different . . ." Ibid.

p. 38, "They asked me if he could act . . ." Andrews, *True Myths: The Life and Times of Arnold Schwarzenegger*, 41.

p. 38, "immense likability," Leamer, *Fantastic: The Life of Arnold Schwarzenegger*, 104.

p. 38, "Arthur Allan Seidelman's direction . . ." John tanley, *Creature Features: The Science Fiction, Fantasy and Horror Movie Guide* (New York: Berkeley Boulevard Books, 2000), 241.

p. 39, "confirms that, then and later . . ." Andrews, *True Myths: The Life and Times of Arnold Schwarzenegger*, 50.

CHAPTER FOUR: *The Terminator*

p. 40-41, "There was a good deal of resistance . . ." Leigh, *Arnold: An Unauthorized Biography*, 122.

p. 41, "He's a sharp, sharp, sharp guy . . ." Ibid. 123.

p. 41, "eccentric mixture of comedy and drama . . ." Leonard Maltin, ed., *Leonard Maltin's 2006 Movie Guide* (New York: Plume, 2005), 1229.

p. 41, "surprisingly good as the muscle man . . ." Charles Moritz, ed., *Current Biography Yearbook 1979* (New York: H.W. Wilson Company, 1979), 340.

p. 43, "[Schwarzenegger] lights up the film . . ." Leigh, *Arnold: An Unauthorized Biography*, 144.

p. 43, "I knew the more outrageous . . ." Leamer, *Fantastic: The Life of Arnold Schwarzenegger*, 135.

p. 44, "It's a typical woman thing . . ." Leamer, *Fantastic: The Life of Arnold Schwarzenegger*, 129.

p. 45, "When he was in town . . ." Leigh, *Arnold: An Unauthorized Biography*, 150.

p. 46, "that's brighter than I . . ." Leamer, *Fantastic: The Life of Arnold Schwarzenegger*, 152.

p. 47, "she always says that the first time . . ." Leamer, *Fantastic: The Life of Arnold Schwarzenegger*, 159.

p. 48, "I had to make a wrenching decision . . ." "Maria Shriver," in *Current Biography Yearbook 1991*, ed. Charles Moritz (New York: H.W. Wilson Company, 1991), 519.

p. 48, "about as emotive as . . ." Leigh, *Arnold: An Unauthorized Biography*, 195.

p. 48, "a dull clod with a sharp sword . . ." Leamer, *Fantastic: The Life of Arnold Schwarzenegger*, 190.

p. 48-49, "I want to entertain more people . . ." Leamer, *Fantastic: The Life of Arnold Schwarzenegger*, 163.

p. 50, "Schwarzenegger is perfectly cast . . ." Maltin, *Leonard Maltin's 2006 Movie Guide*, 1292.

p. 50, "an incredibly satisfying viewing experience . . ." Stanley, Creature Features: *The Science Fiction, Fantasy, and Horror Movie Guide*, 514.

p. 50, "I want to move to America . . ." Leamer, *Fantastic: The Life of Arnold Schwarzenegger*, 215.

p. 51, "Of course, *Rambo* and *Commando* . . ." Leigh, *Arnold: An Unauthorized Biography*, 221.

CHAPTER FIVE: Political Beginnings

p. 52, "We fly back and forth . . ." Leamer, *Fantastic: The Life of Arnold Schwarzenegger*, 237.

p. 53, "You're an expert on . . ." Scott Stossel, *Sarge: The Life of Sargent Shriver* (Washington, D.C.: Smithsonian Books, 2004), 670.

p. 54, "I would sit for hours . . ." Ibid.

p. 54, "I have a love interest . . ." Brandon, *Arnold Schwarzenegger*, 54.

p. 54-55, "My characters just defend themselves . . ." Ibid., 55.

p. 56, "Effectively blends sentiment and roughhouse humor . . ." *Maltin, Leonard Maltin's 2006 Movie Guide*, 1367.

p. 58, "Look, I'm in a sort of difficult situation . . ." *Leamer, Fantastic: The Life of Arnold Schwarzenegger*, 271.

p. 59, "It is strange and bizarre . . ." Andrews, *True Myths The Life and Times of Arnold Schwarzenegger*, 191.

p. 59, "as much about the nature of reality . . ." Ibid.

p. 59, "The story is laid out . . ." C.J. Henderson, *The Encyclopedia of Science Fiction Movies* (New York: Checkmark Books, 2001), 423.

CHAPTER SIX: *Jingle All the Way*

p. 62, "It was supposed to be . . ." Andrews, *True Myths The Life and Times of Arnold Schwarzenegger*, 231.

p. 62-63, "Genuinely bad writing and an overall air . . ." Maltin, *Leonard Maltin's 2006 Movie Guide*, 718.

p. 63, "Precious few laughs . . ." Ibid.

p. 64, "inappropriate," Ibid., 678.

p. 65, "That was another thing . . ." Leamer, *Fantastic: The Life of Arnold Schwarzenegger*, 326.

p. 66, "I urged him to make the race . . ." Leamer, *Fantastic: The Life of Arnold Schwarzenegger*, 329-330.

p. 68, "Idiotic beyond the point of . . ." Leamer, *Fantastic: The Life of Arnold Schwarzenegger*, 322.

p. 68, "sinfully stupid," Ibid.

p. 68, "*End of Days* is dreadful enough . . ." Ibid., 323.

p. 68, "a terrible case of miscasting," Stanley, *Creature Features The Science Fiction, Fantasy and Horror Movie Guide*, 167.

p. 68, "reasonably entertaining," Ted Anthony, "End of Days (1999)," review of "End of Days (1999)," http://www.geocities.com/theactionkings/ActonKings Shwarzenegger-End of Days.html.

p. 70-71, "You read all these commentaries . . ." "Gray Davis," in *Current Biography Yearbook 1999.* (New York: H.W. Wilson Company, 1999), 160.

CHAPTER SEVEN: Recall

p. 74, "We were sitting in the Jacuzzi . . ." Leamer, *Fantastic: The Life of Arnold Schwarzenegger*, 351.

p. 74-75, "It was very tough for her . . ." Ibid.

p. 75, "You know, if I were to run . . ." Ibid., 359.

p. 76, "It is the most difficult decision . . ." Ibid., 362.

p. 76, "The man that is failing the people . . ." Ibid.

p. 77, "I-I will have to get into that . . ." Ibid., 365.

p. 77, "I felt that the campaign needed . . ." Ibid., 366.

p. 78, "When I came to California . . ." Ibid., 372.

p. 78, "What has happened to California . . ." Ibid.

p. 78, "Now I believe that we all . . ." Ibid.

p. 79, "Before the carping begins . . ." Ibid., 373.

p. 80, "I want to thank you . . ." Ibid., 375.

p. 80, "We're going to cover . . ." Ibid., 381

p. 82, "He is arguably the best-known . . ." Ibid., 393.

p. 82, "SIX WOMEN SAY . . ." Ibid., 400.

p. 83, "touched them in a sexual manner . . ." Ibid.

p. 84, "Most people shrugged . . ." Ibid.

p. 84, "A lot of those . . ." Ibid., 402.

p. 84, "And so what I want . . ." Ibid., 402-403.

p. 85, "At a time when . . ." Karen Tumulty,
"The 5 Meanings of Arnold," *Time*, October 20, 2003.

CHAPTER EIGHT: Governor Schwarzenegger

p. 86, "I am humbled . . ." Leamer, *Fantastic: The Life of Arnold Schwarzenegger*, 413.

p. 87, "The election was not about . . ." John M. Broder
and Dean E. Murphy, "Schwarzenegger Takes Oath
and Vows End to Divisions," *New York Times*, November
18, 2003.

p. 89, "expected to wring billions . . ." Leamer, *Fantastic:
The Life of Arnold Schwarzenegger*, 448.

p. 90, "It would have been nice . . ." Ibid., 453.

p. 91, "The debate is over . . ." Thomas Friedman, "Arnold comes
to the rescue," *Sarasota Herald-Tribune*, March 29, 2007.

p. 92, "But we will never change . . ." Christopher Keyes,
"True Colors," *Outside*, April 2007, 68.

p. 95, "If I was to make another Terminator movie . . ."
USA Today, November 10, 2005.

p. 97, "After his historic election . . ." "Schwarzenegger
for Governor," *Los Angeles Times*, October 15, 2006.

Bibliography

Andrews, Nigel. *True Myths The Life and Times of Arnold Schwarzenegger.* Seacaucus, N.J.: Birch Lane Press, 1996.

"Arnie's total recall flawed; Republican convention. *Times* (London, England), September 4, 2004.

"Arnold's Poll Numbers Dip Latest Survey Finds Drop in Popularity Among Democrats, Independents." *Daily News* (Los Angeles, Ca.) September 23, 2004.

Bial, Daniel. *Arnold Schwarzenegger Man of Action.* New York: Franklin Watts, 1998.

Brandon, Karen. *Arnold Schwarzenegger.* San Diego: Lucent Books, 2004.

Duda, Karen E. "Arnold Schwarzenegger." *Current Biography Yearbook* 2004. New York: H.W. Wilson Company, 2004.

Ellis, John. "Governor basks in afterglow Schwarzenegger speech gets high marks from the GOP." *Fresno Bee* (California), September 2, 2004.

"Excerpts From Address By Gov. Schwarzenegger." *New York Times*, September 1, 2004.

Friedman, Thomas. "Arnold comes to the rescue." *Sarasota Herald-Tribune,* March 29, 2007. 11A.

Grover, Ronald, Christopher Palmeri, and Katie Kerwin. "Choose Your Weapon, Arnold." *Business Week*, October 27, 2003.

Grover, Ronald, Christopher Palmeri, and Ben Elgin. "Something's Got to Give." *Business Week*, October 20, 2003.

Henderson, C.J. *The Encyclopedia of Science Fiction Movies.* New York: Checkmark Books, 2001.

Keyes, Christopher. "True Colors". *Outside*, April 2007.

Krugman, Paul. "California's Complications." *Sarasota Herald-Tribune*, January 17, 2007.

Lacayo, Richard. "The Mind Behind the Muscles." *Time*, August 18, 2003.

Laqueur, Walter, ed. *The Holocaust Encyclopedia.*
New Haven, CT: Yale University Press, 2001.
"Is California back? Is California back? American Politics.
(California's Chances of Reform). *Economist,* April 29, 2004.
Leamer, Laurence. *Fantastic The Life of Arnold Schwarzenegger.*
New York: St. Martins Press, 2005.
Leigh, Wendy. *Arnold: An Unauthorized Biography.*
Chicago: Congdon & Weed, Inc., 1990.
Lipsyte, Robert, and Levine, Peter. *Idols of the Game.*
Atlanta: Turner Publishing, Inc., 1995.
Marinucci, Carla, and Martin, Mark. "Schwarzenegger
Re-Elected in Landslide, Weathering Anti-GOP Storm."
San Francisco Chronicle, November 8, 2006.
Moritz, Charles, ed. *Current Biography Yearbook 1991.*
New York: H.W. Wilson Company, 1991.
Schwarzenegger, Arnold, and Douglas Kent Hall. *Arnold:
The Education of a Body Builder.* New York: Simon
and Schuster, 1977.
"Schwarzenegger for Governor." *Los Angeles Times,* October
15, 2006.
Stackman, Michael. "Schwarzenegger Takes to the Limelight
Again." *New York Times,* September 1, 2004.
Stanley, John. *Creature Features The Science Fiction, Fantasy
and Horror Movie Guide.* New York: Berkeley
Boulevard Books, 2000.
Stossel, Scott. *Sarge: The Life and Times of Sargent Shriver.*
Washington, D.C.: Smithsonian Books, 2004.
Tumulty, Karen, and Terry McCarthy. "All That's Missing
Is the Popcorn." *Time,* August 18, 2003.
Tumulty, Karen. "The 5 Meanings of Arnold." *Time,*
October 20, 2003.
Unterburger, Amy L., ed. International Directory of Films
and Filmmakers. Vol. 3.

Web sites

http://www.gov.ca.gov
The official Web site of Governor Arnold Schwarzenegger offers the latest news on the governor and his administration.

http://www.joinarnold.com
Paid for by Californians for Schwarzenegger 2006, this site features a campaign slide show, and a slide show of the governor's inaugural ceremony, including photos of his wife, Maria, and their four children. You'll also find links to related sites, such as a link to the governor's office and one on which supporters can make donations.

http://www.schwarzenegger.com
Information about movies in which Schwarzenegger starred, as well as photos and souvenirs, are featured on this Web site.

Index